P9-DGW-788

THE ROAD TO
FREEDOM

THE ROAD TO
FREEDOM

healing from your hurts, hang-ups, and habits

JOHNNY BAKER

ZONDERVAN

ZONDERVAN

The Road to Freedom
Copyright © 2018 by Johnny Baker

Requests for information should be addressed to:
Zondervan, *3900 Sparks Dr. SE, Grand Rapids, Michigan 49546*

ISBN 978-0-310-34987-7 (hardcover)

ISBN 978-0-310-35393-5 (international trade paper edition)

ISBN 978-0-310-34990-7 (audio)

ISBN 978-0-310-34988-4 (ebook)

Scripture quotations are taken from The Holy Bible, New International Version®, NIV®. Copyright © 1973, 1978, 1984, 2011 by Biblica, Inc.® Used by permission of Zondervan. All rights reserved worldwide. www.Zondervan.com. The "NIV" and "New International Version" are trademarks registered in the United States Patent and Trademark Office by Biblica, Inc.™

Any Internet addresses (websites, blogs, etc.) and telephone numbers in this book are offered as a resource. They are not intended in any way to be or imply an endorsement by Zondervan, nor does Zondervan vouch for the content of these sites and numbers for the life of this book.

All rights reserved. No part of this publication may be reproduced, stored in a retrieval system, or transmitted in any form or by any means—electronic, mechanical, photocopy, recording, or any other—except for brief quotations in printed reviews, without the prior permission of the publisher.

Cover design: Studio Gearbox
Cover photo: Blue Collectors / Stocksy
Interior design: Denise Froehlich

First printing April 2018 / Printed in the United States of America

R0452387232

Contents

Foreword

In 1991, when Celebrate Recovery started, Johnny was just fourteen years old. He was supportive and encouraging from the beginning. For several years, he helped me pick up the sound equipment and set up our meeting place. At that time, he was quite confident that he would never need Celebrate Recovery, and part of me prayed that this would be so.

However, Johnny took his own journey and discovered, like his father, that he needed to work the Eight Recovery Principles and the Twelve Steps. Having worked the program in the early years, he knew just where to go to deal with his hurts, hang-ups, and habits as an adult.

While he was new in recovery, my wife, Cheryl, and I began to pray that Johnny would become a leader in the program. God so often answers our prayers in ways far exceeding our plans. In November 2004, Johnny joined Celebrate Recovery's staff at Saddleback Church. His first job was answering phones and doing other administrative responsibilities. He became a leader and completed several Step Studies, and in 2012 he moved into the position of Saddleback's Pastor for Celebrate Recovery.

As Johnny's leadership skills grew, so did his responsibilities. He also serves as the National Team leader and is a favorite speaker at all our training events. His wife, Jeni, has joined him in helping to lead this ministry. I know the future of Celebrate Recovery is in solid, loving hands.

I also know that you will love this book. Johnny will take you through his journey and tell you about many of the life-changing lessons he has learned along the way.

I am so proud to be writing this foreword for his first book. But more important, I am proud to be his father and friend.

—John Baker Sr., pastor and
cofounder of Celebrate Recovery

Introduction

There's a joke in my family that my parents have three kids. First is the oldest, Laura. Then there's me, the middle child. And then there's the baby and the favorite, Celebrate Recovery. Like all good jokes, there is a part of the joke that is true. Celebrate Recovery is my parents' favorite.

Not really.

The true part is that Celebrate Recovery is a "child" of my parents, and in many ways it feels more like a sibling than anything else. Like a sibling, I watched it come into the world through mysterious means. I watched it grow, and I'm proud of what it has become. Unlike a sibling, Celebrate Recovery has never broken one of my toys or blamed me when my parents caught it doing something it shouldn't.

I watched in 1990 when my parents reconciled and began creating Celebrate Recovery. It was a weird and wonderful time for us. I was fourteen and a freshman in high school. Earlier that year, my parents had begun healing their marriage after a thirteen-month separation. What happened in such a condensed amount of time is nothing short of miraculous. No one saw Celebrate Recovery coming.

If you had been in the Baker house a few months before my parents got back together, you wouldn't have predicted they would begin a ministry that would grow into the worldwide movement it is today. If you were among the forty-three people who attended the first Celebrate Recovery meeting at Saddleback Church on November 21, 1991, which was held in a psychiatric hospital's gym, since Saddleback didn't have any land or buildings yet, you wouldn't have seen it coming either. None of us did.

Years later, what started as a ministry for people in our church like my dad and our family has grown into a worldwide movement of God that is now in more than twenty-nine thousand churches all over the world and with materials translated into more than twenty languages. The story of John and Cheryl Baker can't be removed from the story of Celebrate Recovery. Not only has what they started saved and changed the lives of millions of people all over the world, but it also saved and changed mine.

This isn't so much a history of Celebrate Recovery as it is an introduction to what I have learned in the more than twenty-five years that Celebrate Recovery has been part of my life.

I've been involved with the ministry on four levels. First, I was there when Celebrate Recovery was born, and

I was one of the first participants as a teenager. Second, I supported my parents from a distance while they grew Celebrate Recovery, but I was not active or attending and was practicing my addiction. Third, I again became a participant, then a staff member, and eventually the pastor of our local Celebrate Recovery at Saddleback Church. Fourth, I now serve on the National Leadership Team. During those twenty-five years, I gained a unique perspective on the ministry of Celebrate Recovery and learned, firsthand and by watching thousands of lives change, some incredible lessons from it.

"We'll Call It Celebrate Recovery!"

I remember the night as if it were yesterday. My dad and I were sitting in our living room having huge bowls of vanilla ice cream covered in hot caramel sauce. Just a few months earlier, my dad was living in an apartment in Los Angeles after deciding to leave when my mom gave him an ultimatum. They got in a fight over going out for a piece of pie with friends, and in the heat of the moment, my mom yelled, "Either go get counseling with me or get out!" To our surprise, he left.

We spent the next few months in shock and tried to figure out what to do. I'm not sure whether their separation was harder for me or for my friends to handle. For years, my family had been the normal one because my parents were still married. I remember going to school as a freshman and telling my friends I didn't think my parents were going to stay married. Judging by the looks on their faces, you would have thought I had kicked their puppy.

It was a tough time for our family, and it was the excuse I needed to rebel and experiment with girls and drugs. Among my friends, a separation was all the reason you needed to go wild. To be fair, I didn't really need the fuel—I was ready and willing—but the trouble at home gave me the justification to act out. I began smoking weed and lost my virginity at age fourteen. This was the beginning of some patterns that would be tough to break for decades.

Meanwhile, in his apartment in Los Angeles, my dad had begun attending Alcoholics Anonymous. He later told us that losing his family was the catalyst he needed to take a close look at his life and make some big changes. He attended more than ninety meetings in ninety days and worked hard on his recovery with his sponsor. Little by little, my parents reconciled. First with some calls, then with some conversations when he picked us kids up or dropped us off, and eventually a lunch date on Valentine's Day. My dad is smooth.

At that lunch, my dad made his amends to my mom. He said he was sorry for his part in their damaged relationship and asked her for forgiveness. I will never be able to thank

God enough that my mom accepted his apology and began forgiving him. I will also never forget the moment he made similar amends to me.

I sat on his bed while he sat next to me in a recliner, and he told me he was an alcoholic and apologized to me for breaking our family. I remember trying to tell him I didn't think he was an alcoholic. I said I never saw him drunk; he just drank beer until he fell asleep. He asked me if I thought that was normal. I said, "Yes?" He told me it wasn't; most people don't drink beer for breakfast or choose to leave when their wives ask them to go out for pie. He asked for my forgiveness, and I said I forgave him before the words left his mouth.

Eventually, my parents completely reconciled, and they even renewed their wedding vows, with my sister as maid of honor and me as best man. Their marriage was made new. A partnership was formed between the two of them as my dad continued to work his recovery through AA. After moving back into the house, my dad did something we never saw coming. He asked to go to church with us. My sister and I had given up inviting him years earlier when we got good at predicting his excuses. So his asking to come with us was new.

He came that weekend to Saddleback Church and heard Pastor Rick Warren speak. He had the experience many of us have had, when it feels like Pastor Rick is speaking directly to us. On that Sunday, my dad heard the message and something stirred inside of him. Years earlier, my dad had resisted the call to ministry because he never felt good enough to be a pastor. That Sunday, God called John Baker to fulfill what he had put on his heart decades ago. Things were about to change again.

Soon after that Sunday, my dad threw himself back into his relationship with Jesus. When he began attending AA, he knew who his higher power was and that he had a name, Jesus Christ. But as he drew closer to Jesus, he found opposition in his AA groups when he tried to share about him. I understand this is not everyone's experience, but it was his. In his particular AA groups, he felt uncomfortable sharing about Jesus as his higher power and had some people flat-out tell him he was not allowed to do so.

Meanwhile, in the men's ministry small groups he attended at church, he felt that the men in his groups were not ready or willing to go as deep as he needed to in their sharing when he tried to talk about his struggle with alcohol. Every week, he attended Saddleback and looked around at the many people who attended. Saddleback had around six thousand in weekly worship service attendance, and he knew that he could not be the only one struggling with an addiction.

So he did the obvious thing. He sat down and wrote Pastor Rick a short, concise, thirteen-page, single-spaced letter outlining the vision for Celebrate Recovery. I say he wrote the letter, but really what he did was dictate to my mom, who sat at a typewriter (if you don't know what a typewriter is, ask someone over thirty) to help him get his ideas on paper. He confidently mailed the letter to Pastor Rick and believed that once he read it, Pastor Rick would find just the right man to lead this ministry.

A few days later, my dad found himself in Pastor Rick's office. Pastor Rick said, "John, I read your letter. It sounds great. Do it!" Just like that, Celebrate Recovery was born.

During the writing of the letter, I spent a lot of time with my dad as he dreamed of what the ministry would be like. One night he said, "I came up with a name! We'll call it Celebrate Recovery!" I said, "Father! That sounds amazing! Celebrate Recovery will surely change the world!"

Probably not.

As a fifteen-year-old, I probably rolled my eyes and grunted. At the time, I didn't really understand the name. What was there to celebrate in recovery? To me, it sounded pretty dreary. Don't get me wrong, I was glad it brought my dad back, but sitting in a circle and talking about your feelings? Hard pass. But my dad was back and was so excited about it. I just said, "Cool," and figured my part was pretty much done.

Things didn't quite work out that way. I was "invited" by my parents to attend Celebrate Recovery every Friday night. For some reason, they didn't think it was a good idea to leave me home alone every week. So I became the first setup and tear-down team member. Each week, my dad and I borrowed the church van, lovingly nicknamed the Pumpkin Van (I'll let you guess what color it was), and filled it up with chairs and sound equipment. We drove to Charter Hospital and set up Celebrate Recovery in the gym. The first week, forty-three people attended, and it grew steadily during the following months.

I also became the first leader of the teens' recovery group. This was a loose group of the kids whose parents also had the wisdom not to trust them to be alone on Friday nights. A better name for our group would have been the "complain about your parents group," since that's what we did with most of our time. Let me just say that this group would not be allowed in Celebrate Recovery today. We broke about every small group guideline there is, including meeting as a coed group.

That season was an incredible one for the ministry and for my family. We took our church's membership, maturity, and ministry classes together and got baptized in a backyard swimming pool together. I got deeply involved in our high school ministry, and my sister and I watched as our parents grew closer together and closer to Christ in ways we never imagined. Men and women began coming to them for help and counsel and sought my parents' advice. My dad began to write and teach the recovery lessons, and we watched as he stood in front of the group, dry-mouthed and nervous, and laid the foundation for Celebrate Recovery. The very first lives changed by Celebrate Recovery were ours.

The Road to Recovery

As Pastor Rick watched lives being changed in Celebrate Recovery, he studied the Twelve Steps of AA and found that they reminded him of something: the Beatitudes. The Twelve Steps echo what Christ said in the Sermon on the Mount. Pastor Rick studied them together and developed the Eight Recovery Principles. They are:

- Principle 1: Realize I'm not God; I admit that I am powerless to control my tendency to do the wrong thing and that my life is unmanageable.
  "Happy are those who know that they are spiritually poor."
- Principle 2: Earnestly believe that God exists, that I matter to him, and that he has the power to help me recover.
  "Happy are those who mourn, for they shall be comforted."
- Principle 3: Consciously choose to commit all my life and will to Christ's care and control.
  "Happy are the meek."

- Principle 4: Openly examine and confess my faults to myself, to God, and to someone I trust.

  "Happy are the pure in heart."

- Principle 5: Voluntarily submit to any and all changes God wants to make in my life and humbly ask him to remove my character defects.

  "Happy are those whose greatest desire is to do what God requires."

- Principle 6: Evaluate all my relationships. Offer forgiveness to those who have hurt me and make amends for harm I've done to others when possible, except when to do so would harm them or others.

  "Happy are the merciful."

  "Happy are the peacemakers."

- Principle 7: Reserve a time with God for self-examination, Bible reading, and prayer in order to know God and his will for my life and to gain the power to follow his will.

- Principle 8: Yield myself to God to be used to bring this Good News to others, both by my example and my words.

  "Happy are those who are persecuted because they do what God requires."

In 1993, Pastor Rick took our entire church through an eight-week sermon series called "The Road to Recovery," in which he went over each of these recovery principles. After that, Celebrate Recovery really took off. The weekly meetings grew as more people realized a powerful truth: Celebrate Recovery is not just for people with drug and alcohol problems. There has been a misconception about this since the beginning, so let me be clear: Celebrate Recovery is not just for people with drug and alcohol problems. Celebrate Recovery is for anyone with a hurt, hang-up, or habit.

When Pastor Rick took our church through "The Road to Recovery," thousands of people saw that recovery was for them. He made recovery safe and acceptable for people in our church and community. Pastor Rick's support and passion for Celebrate Recovery made our church a safe place.

Unfortunately, my involvement with Celebrate Recovery shifted at this time. I went from an active and usually willing participant to a cheerleader on the sidelines. I watched as my parents grew this ministry and impacted hundreds of lives at our church. I was still active in the youth ministry at Saddleback and had completed a Step Study with a mentor and friend of mine, but I decided Celebrate Recovery was my parents' thing.

I was so proud of them, and I listened as they told me stories of the men and women who came through the ministry. My dad was unrecognizable. He went from an active alcoholic to pastor on staff at Saddleback in a way that can only be described as miraculous. The change was total and complete. He was a new man. He grew in his teaching and writing, and he created tools and resources to help people systematically move through the recovery principles.

Celebrate Recovery spread into other churches all over the United States. People heard about Celebrate Recovery and wanted it at their church. The participant's guides my dad wrote were self-published, and we sold them from our garage. My parents would go to a post-office box to get the orders, and were able to see how and where Celebrate Recovery was growing.

In 2001, just a few weeks after 9/11, my parents were invited to share about Celebrate Recovery at a church in Annapolis, Maryland. My sister and I weren't thrilled with their traveling so close to the tragedy. But they felt this might be the one and only time they would be asked to teach other churches how to start Celebrate Recovery. They were wrong. Since 2001, they have done well over two hundred of these one-day training events. A great joy of my life is that I have been able to join them since being added to the Saddleback staff in 2004. But that's getting ahead of myself.

Walking Away and Coming Back Home

During this time of growth for the ministry, I went through hard times. Convinced I would not repeat my dad's mistakes,

I began drinking alcohol with friends. I had avoided this behavior in high school, but as I got older, I believed I would be able to handle it. At first, I did. I drank occasionally with friends. But those occasions became more and more frequent.

I quickly developed a taste and a tolerance for alcohol and drank only to get drunk. Soon I was drinking daily. I hid this behavior from all but a crew of drinking buddies and led a double life, continuing to volunteer at church in visible roles while secretly drinking to excess. I believed I was fooling everyone, but I learned I wasn't. People were on to me. A great source of shame for me was the embarrassment I must have caused my parents.

In December 1999, I called my dad from jail when I was arrested for driving under the influence of alcohol. That call was one of the hardest I have ever had to make. After all, I was calling not just my dad but also the founder and pastor of Celebrate Recovery! He was so gracious with me. He told me to sit tight and he'd work on it. He could have yelled, but he didn't. He could have lectured me or told me I'd rot in jail before he bailed me out, but he didn't.

When I was released, he was there with a hug and told me I needed to take a look at my actions, but he left it up to me. He was amazing. I was convinced my fiancée would call off our upcoming wedding, but she didn't. She was also gracious and kind and forgiving. I didn't deserve either response, but I was favored with them.

Although this moment was a low one for me, it wasn't enough for me to stop drinking. I was in denial, and thanks to my lawyer, I could blame the officers for doing things they weren't supposed to. I blamed my circumstances instead of myself. I continued to drink for another four years, although I never drove under the influence again.

When Jeni and I got married, I amped up the secrecy. I lied to her about the extent of my drinking and did many sneaky things to hide my addiction. I had moments of clarity, but I pushed them away with ferocity to protect my habit and my secret. My addiction began to isolate me from my most important relationships. I hid my drinking and lied to Jeni, I felt guilty around my recovery superstar parents, and I drank alone. It wasn't a party anymore. Drinking had become medicine.

Jeni became pregnant with our first daughter, Maggie, in 2003, and we were so excited. But as I thought about my impending fatherhood, drinking became less and less fun. I didn't want my kids to grow up with an alcoholic dad the way I did. As I said earlier, my dad was never violent or hurtful in his addiction, but he was unavailable. I had done enough work in recovery to know I didn't want to be unavailable to my children. I knew I needed to stop, but I didn't know how.

You would think that with the recovery experts a phone call away, I'd put two and two together, but I didn't.

I thought I needed to do it on my own. I did the typical thing of pouring out all of the alcohol in my house, and I told Jeni I thought I was an alcoholic. I stopped drinking long before Maggie was born, but I thought about it all the time. When Maggie arrived and had a hard time sleeping or cried a lot, I fantasized about escaping with alcohol. One hot night as I was taking out the trash, I stood outside and had to fight the urge to drive to the store to buy something to drink. I knew I needed help. I reached out to my dad and began my third phase of involvement with Celebrate Recovery: attending groups to deal with my alcohol issues.

Something strange happened as I applied the recovery principles to my life: I changed. As I grew in my recovery, I felt called to enter ministry. I was not excited about this. At the time, I was a manager in a restaurant and considered entering culinary school. My dream was to own a restaurant, and ministry was not part of that plan.

One day on my way to work, I felt God plainly call me into ministry. So I did the only natural thing: I turned off the radio. It was as if I thought the call had come from there. I yelled, "No!" I was fine where I was; I had a career and a baby at home. But God turned up the volume of his call, and everyone I talked to, every single one of them, confirmed that call and told me to take the next step.

I applied for several jobs at Saddleback and was told no at every turn. God closed door after door until finally I thought I had misheard him. Eventually, after I told my dad I had been turned down for another opportunity, Dad asked if I would ever consider working for Celebrate Recovery. I practically shouted, "Yes!" before he could get the words out. We both wanted it, but we both wanted it to be the other's idea. Little did I know that my parents and my sister had been praying for years for me to want to work for Celebrate Recovery. I began in November 2004.

At that point, Celebrate Recovery was growing at a mind-racing pace, blossoming into a worldwide movement of God. Thousands of churches had begun Celebrate Recovery ministries, and hundreds of thousands of people had found freedom and victory from all kinds of hurts, hang-ups, or habits. My parents were gone at least twice a month presenting those one-day training events, the ones they thought they would never get to do again, while I stayed home and helped with the day-to-day, back-end operations of the ministry, learning a lot from the other staff and leaders. As I continued attending Celebrate Recovery for my issues, I also started answering phone calls and emails about Celebrate Recovery that came in from around the world. Celebrate Recovery was now a daily part of my life. My work was Celebrate Recovery, my family all talked about and participated in Celebrate Recovery, and I continued to work out my issues in Celebrate Recovery. It was all-consuming and immersive.

After a time, I began leading groups at Celebrate Recovery and got to have a front-row seat to others' life changes. Little by little, I took on more responsibilities. Some of them were so subtle I missed them, or at least I don't remember saying yes to them, while others were intentional. Not everyone at Celebrate Recovery at Saddleback was thrilled about my involvement. I can't say I blame them, and I worked hard to earn their approval.

Some of them eventually did accept me, while others did not. I'm still codependent enough to admit that this hurts. Some of the leaders at Saddleback left as I took on more roles. It was hard to watch, but it taught me a great lesson. This one doesn't count as one of the Ten Life Lessons coming up; let's call it a bonus. Here it is: not everyone is going to like you.

I spent a few years fighting for acceptance at our home group while I traveled with the one-day team and taught the key principles of Celebrate Recovery to other churches. It took me longer than I'd like to admit to learn this lesson, but I finally did. It's a good thing I did too, because in 2012, I became the pastor of Celebrate Recovery at Saddleback Church. I became licensed and oversaw the ministry while my dad focused on the global growth of Celebrate Recovery.

I am now in my fourth stage of involvement with Celebrate Recovery. Not only am I part of the national leadership team, but I am a traveling speaker, an author of

Celebrate Recovery resources, and the Celebrate Recovery pastor at Saddleback. In addition, my wife, Jeni, and I serve together in ministry, carrying on the tradition that my parents started of working side by side. Jeni is on the national team and leads Celebrate Recovery Step Study groups for pastors' wives at our church. It is a blessing for me to serve with her and to see our lives and our marriage so transformed.

I have watched Celebrate Recovery go from an idea in my father's mind to a ministry in more than twenty-nine thousand churches all over the world. I have seen it grow through the efforts of men and women who serve as leaders and pastors in local Celebrate Recovery ministries or who volunteer as state representatives, regional directors, and members of the national team. All this has been done through the power of Jesus Christ. The term *viral* has come to mean something different in our social-media society, but Celebrate Recovery has truly grown in a viral way. As one person has his or her life changed by Jesus through Celebrate Recovery, they "infect" others in their community and family when they invite them to experience the same change. More than 3.5 million people have gone through a Celebrate Recovery Step Study, and the number is growing every day.

My privileged access to Celebrate Recovery, from sharing dreams over bowls of ice cream, to setting up and tearing down, to willing and sometimes unwilling participant, to sideline cheerleader, to desperate addict needing recovery, to staff member and eventually pastor, has given me insight into some incredible life lessons these past twenty-five years. I'm sharing this not because I'm special but because I've been given a special view of Celebrate Recovery from the beginning.

My life was changed over and over because of Celebrate Recovery, and I have watched thousands of other lives change right in front of my eyes. I've learned these lessons both first- and secondhand and have come to know that these Ten Life Lessons (far from the only ten things to learn) are applicable to anyone, whether or not they will ever set foot in a Celebrate Recovery circle. Learning these lessons will help anyone either start or grow deeper in their recovery journey.

If you are in Celebrate Recovery, you have probably learned many of these lessons already. It's my hope to shine some new light on them and help you as you take your recovery to the next level. If you're not in Celebrate Recovery, I hope you'll learn from those of us who are. I'll also be praying that you decide to check out Celebrate Recovery for yourself. I know you'll find help with the things that are tying you up or slowing you down.

Remember that Celebrate Recovery isn't just for drug addicts and alcoholics. Only a third of the people who attend Celebrate Recovery are struggling with drug addiction or alcoholism. If over the course of these pages you are inspired to check out Celebrate Recovery for yourself, please visit www.celebraterecovery.com and click on the tab labeled "How do I find a Celebrate Recovery" to locate Celebrate Recovery ministries in your area.

Even if you never set foot in a Celebrate Recovery meeting (though I think everyone should), in these pages I'll pass along some of the lessons I have learned, lessons that apply not just to recovery or to those who are in recovery but to all areas of life.

Let's get started.

Admitting you have a problem doesn't make you weak

This is where it all begins. To change in any area, we must first admit we have a problem. In recovery we call this coming out of denial, which means we realize that things in our lives are out of control and unmanageable. It's right there in the first of the eight Celebrate Recovery principles. Principle 1 says, "Realize I'm not God. I admit that I am powerless to control my tendency to do the wrong thing and that my life is unmanageable." This is the beginning of the journey.

But for many of us, myself included, this step is easier said than done. None of us likes to admit we have problems.

It's easy to point at the addict and say, "Well, obviously her life is a mess!" But it's much harder to look at the image in the mirror and say the same thing. We have bought the lie that to be strong, we have to have it all together. And the first step in having it all together is making sure we never even appear to be out of control.

Then we look at our bank accounts and we see major debt with no way to get out. We look at our scales and see our weight creeping up year after year. We look at our sons and daughters and wish we could help them avoid the mistakes we made when we were their age. We fear that someone will find our browser history and find out what we've been looking at online. We worry that someone will see us tear up for no good reason and find out we've been battling depression. We pull up to church fighting with our family and yell, "We're at church! Pull it together! These people think we're normal!"

So if this is universal, if we all have these kinds of issues, shouldn't it be easy to admit it? We all know that it's not.

Over the years, Celebrate Recovery ministries have begun in almost every major Christian denomination and in prisons, military bases, youth homes, and recovery centers. Every state in America has at least one Celebrate Recovery ministry, and most have many more. But from time to time, we're told, "Well, I don't think Celebrate Recovery will work in [insert specific culture, people group, or geographic region], because people in my [specific culture, people group, or geographic region] don't talk openly about our issues." You know what's funny? We've heard that about pretty much every culture, people group, or geographic region. There's a simple reason why: talking about our issues isn't normal.

Normal People

Normal people keep their issues to themselves. Normal people don't admit they need help. Normal people don't talk about what's wrong. You know who does? *Those* people. You know *those* people, don't you? Yeah. Them. Those people are the ones who talk about stuff you're supposed to keep to yourself. Those people seek help when they need it instead of pretending everything is okay. Those people are filling our Celebrate Recovery groups and counselor's offices and support groups all around the world. And those people are getting better.

Now, if you're a normal person, don't worry about it; what *those* people know is that you have issues too. The truth about those people is that we were once normal too. You wouldn't know it by looking at some of us, but we were. Then something happened. Something big that caused us to look over at those people and say, "I want that." It was scary for us; none of us wanted to do it. We were fine with normal, but the situations we found ourselves in wouldn't allow us to stay normal.

You may have heard this referred to as hitting rock bottom or having a moment of clarity. However you refer to it, the result is the same: something makes it impossible to ignore the problem. My wife was pregnant with our first child, and suddenly I couldn't pretend my drinking wasn't a problem any longer. This little baby was going to change everything, and I didn't want to carry my baggage into fatherhood. I couldn't pretend everything was okay anymore.

In the Bible, David had this kind of moment. He said, "When I kept silent, my bones wasted away through my groaning all day long. For day and night your hand was heavy on me; my strength was sapped as in the heat of summer. Then I acknowledged my sin to you and did not cover up my iniquity. I said, 'I will confess my transgressions to the LORD.' And you forgave the guilt of my sin" (Ps. 32:3–5).

David knew what it's like to try to keep sins, out-of-control behavior, or what we in Celebrate Recovery call hurts, hang-ups, and habits a secret. Maybe you can identify with the first part of that verse. Maybe you have tried to deny that you have pain or that something in your life is out of whack, and you've felt that wasting, groaning, strength-sapping feeling David felt. You've experienced a moment of clarity.

God will use pain to get your attention. Notice how

David says, "For day and night your hand was heavy on me." David is talking about the hand of God. He's saying that God put the pressure on him and wouldn't let up. C. S. Lewis wrote, "Pain insists upon being attended to. God whispers to us in our pleasures, speaks in our consciences, but shouts in our pains. It is his megaphone to rouse a deaf world." In recovery, we have found this to be true. When God wants to get our attention, he uses pain. So when we find ourselves in pain, we have two options. First (spoiler alert: this is the right option), we can turn from our pain to God. Or second, we can allow the pain to grow and get worse and worse.

I hate going to the dentist. Hate. It. If you are a dentist or a dental assistant or anything like that, I'm sure you are a fine person, but one of my main goals in life is never to see you in your office. I hate everything about going to the dentist. I hate the smell of the office. I hate that little light they shine in your face. I hate the metal tools they use to dig around in your mouth. I especially hate the flossing lecture. Look, I'm never going to floss. It hasn't happened yet; I think we can pretty much write it off.

But sometimes I have to go to the dentist. Not every six months for scheduled checkups (I'm pretty sure that's a little joke they tell. Who does that?), but only when I am in pain. Not the little pain a few ibuprofen a day can take care of, but the knee-buckling, earth-shattering, "why did God even put nerves in our teeth in the first place?" kind of pain. Then, and only then, will I go to the dentist. Sometimes they can save a tooth or do a few things to take the pain away, but sometimes they have to do a root canal. The devil invented root canals. What do you think gnashing of teeth means? If I went to the dentist every six months like they say you're supposed to, they would catch problems before they caused pain. They'd be less expensive and the treatment would be less painful. But I don't. I wait and I wait until the pain is unbearable.

Go ahead and judge me, but many of us do the same thing with the pain in our lives. We see that our marriages could use some work, but we decide we'd rather avoid a fight. And the pain gets worse. We say we are going to change this time for real, but we find ourselves right back in the old behavior. And the pain gets worse. We wish we could stand up for ourselves against the bullies in our families, but we are too afraid. It "isn't that big of a deal," so we stay silent. And the pain gets worse. I don't know what causes you pain, but I do know that left untreated, it will get worse.

First Steps

So where do we begin? We come out of denial. Coming out of denial means admitting our pain. We haven't fixed anything yet, but we have taken the first step to finding the change we need. In his book *Life's Healing Choices*, Pastor John Baker (my father) puts it this way: "To deny your pain is to refuse God's power to help you recover. You will never find healing from your hurts, hang-ups, and habits until you confront your pain."

Pretending to have it all together may feel like strength. We put self-reliant people on a pedestal and respect people who can pull themselves up by their bootstraps. There's a problem with this kind of thinking. Our power is limited. When we try to resolve our problems on our own or when we pretend we don't have problems in the first place, we will run out of the energy we need to sustain that change or preserve that illusion.

God's power is infinite. He can do all things, and he can give us the power to do all things. Philippians 4:13 says, "For I can do everything through Christ, who gives me strength" (NLT). Notice, the verse says that *Christ* gives us strength. The strength doesn't come from within us; it comes from *him*.

I love gadgets. I'm hooked on my smartphone and tablet. I use them all day, every day. No matter how good the batteries are, no matter how advanced the technology, at some point the power inside the gadgets runs out and they need to be plugged in. You and I are the same way. You have strengths inside of you, and the temptation is to live on your own power, but eventually your power will run out. It might last several days or weeks or a year, but it will run out. You need a power greater than your own.

And there is no power greater than Jesus.

The Bible says this about Jesus: "Through him all things were made; without him nothing was made that has been made. In him was life, and that life was the light of all mankind" (John 1:3–4). That's power.

There's a Sunday school song that kids have sung for generations called "He's Got the Whole World in His Hands." It's one of those songs that once you're reminded of it, you wind up humming it all day. (You're welcome.) It's a cute song that we sing with kids to show them that God has everything in control.

But as adults, we think that some things *aren't* in his hands. We think we probably need to handle things that are too big or too small for God. We have to hold it all together. We try to do things on our own power.

One of my favorite exchanges in the Bible is in the book of Job. Job was a man who was faithful to God in a time when most men were faithless. Satan approached the throne of God and said that Job was faithful only because God had blessed him. So God gave Satan permission to destroy Job's life to see if he proved to be faithful. Job lost everything. He lost his riches, his family, and even his health. Job's wife tried to convince him to curse God and then die, but Job remained faithful. He did ask God some tough questions, though, and he did complain. And God responded, "Where were you when I laid the earth's foundation? Tell me, if you understand. Who marked off its dimensions? Surely you know! Who stretched a measuring line across it? On what were its footings set, or who laid its cornerstone—while the morning stars sang together and all the angels shouted for joy?" (Job 38:4–7).

That Sunday school song doesn't seem so silly now, does it? God created the universe. The Genesis account in the Bible says that God spoke the world into existence. He said words and the universe came to life. I don't know about you, but I've never said, "Let there be sandwich," and ended up with anything but an empty stomach. But God has power we can never understand. When you admit you have problems, when you admit that things are out of control and you need help, it doesn't mean you are weak. Admitting your problems trades your power for God's. And God has tremendous power.

So what do you do? How do you admit you need help?

First, admit it to yourself.

It might seem like the first step should be to admit it to God. We'll get there. But first you have to admit it to yourself. There has to be a moment when you say, "Enough!"

It might be as you look over the bills and finally admit you need to get on a budget. It could be you are tired of feeling the shame of losing your temper with your kids. You may realize that a loved one will never meet your expectations. You may find that you aren't just sad but that you are actually depressed. Maybe you see that in order to have someone love you, you said yes ten times this week to things you should have said no to. It could be that you are tired of starving yourself to achieve unattainable perfection. You may be tired of carrying around bitterness over hurts and anger. Whatever your situation is, you have to admit to yourself that you have a hurt in your life and you don't know what to do with it.

After I got my DUI, I had to attend some court-ordered alcohol-awareness classes, in addition to my mandated recovery meetings. Every week, I'd go to a classroom where we'd watch videos about the dangers of drunk driving and hear from police officers and other officials about what would happen the next time we got arrested. I hated it.

I had all kinds of excuses for why I got arrested that night, lots of reasons why it wasn't my fault. I was in denial, and so I did everything I could to justify my actions and pretend that I didn't have a problem with alcohol. I certainly didn't need to be in this group! Every week I'd leave and feel so high and mighty about myself. After all, I had only one DUI; most of these guys were on their second or third. There was even one man who had just received his fourth DUI charge. *Those* guys had problems; I was fine.

One week during the group session, the leader shared that the day he said he was an alcoholic was the most freeing day of his life. He said that in that moment, he knew he never had to drink again. I remember sitting there in my denial, my hat pulled down over my eyes, arms folded, and silent, thinking, *Where's the freedom in that? If I ever say I'm an alcoholic, I'll never be able to drink again.* There wasn't any freedom in that admission for me yet.

Because I was unwilling to admit I had a problem, I continued my out-of-control drinking for another four years. Once I was finally ready to admit to myself I had a problem, I was able to move forward.

The next step is to ask God for help.

Remind yourself about God's power. When you admit you need help, you trade your limited power for God's unlimited power. That means you now have the power to overcome your problem. Jesus said, "With man this is impossible, but with God all things are possible" (Matt. 19:26). All things.

What does that leave out? Overcoming your hurts, hang-ups, or habits is covered by "all things." The big scary things you don't want to look at? Yes, they're in there too. Oh, wait, the details—God can't possibly help with the details! He's so big there's no way he can care about the little things.

No, I think the details are "all things" too.

What Keeps Us from Turning to God?

Many people have been able to admit to themselves they have a problem, but they aren't able to turn to God for help. I think that's for three main reasons: we think we should do it ourselves, we don't understand who God is, and we're afraid God will let us down. Let's look at each of those reasons.

1. We Think We Should Do It Ourselves

There is a myth that heroes are the people who are able to take care of themselves. The self-made and self-reliant are idolized, and we are told, "Be like them!" This thinking keeps us stuck in our helplessness, especially when we realize that we don't have the power we thought we had. But we tell ourselves we should be able to change on our own, that if we tried hard enough or wanted it enough, we'd make it.

"Wanted it enough" is a phrase that drives me crazy. I hear it all the time watching sports. An announcer will say, "It all comes down to the team that wants it more." Really? So, in the Super Bowl, the difference is desire? It seems to me when there are high stakes, both teams want it pretty badly. The same is true for us. You may want to change, but do you have the power to change? All the desire in the world won't change us.

When I was active in my alcoholism, I would come

home from a night out drinking, and as the room spun around me, I'd tell myself that this was the last time. I'd promise myself and I'd promise God that I would change. I had desire. What I didn't have was power. I made God promises, but I forgot to take him up on his promises. I told him what I would do, but I never asked for help. I was the one who would change; I just needed God to back me up. The problem is this: "With man this is impossible, but with God all things are possible" (Matt. 19:26). As long as we are determined to rely on ourselves, we cannot rely on God.

2. We Don't Understand Who God Is

Sometimes we don't turn to God because we don't know who he is. That could be you as you read this. You may be thinking, *That's what the Bible says? So what?* For those of us who have trusted Jesus with our lives, the Bible is the book we go to for help and to better understand who God is. A lot of people call the Bible, "God's instruction book" or a blueprint for life.

I think both of those descriptions are right. The Bible is the best place to learn about who God says he is. The absolute best picture of God was shown in the person of Jesus. The Bible says everything was made in, through, and for Jesus (John 1:3–4). In John 1:1, we are told that Jesus has been with God since the beginning and that he is God. Jesus did something wonderful: he stepped out of heaven and walked among us. "[Jesus], being in very nature God, did not consider equality with God something to be used to his own advantage; rather, he made himself nothing by taking the very nature of a servant, being made in human likeness. And being found in appearance as a man, he humbled himself by becoming obedient to death—even death on a cross!" (Phil. 2:5–8).

Jesus chose to become one of us and died for each and every one of us. The most famous verse in the Bible is John 3:16. It says, "For God so loved the world that he gave his one and only Son, that whoever believes in him shall not perish but have eternal life." This verse reveals so much about who God is—that he is a God who loves us and who gave his Son, Jesus, to die for us and to give us life.

If you don't have a relationship with Jesus, then you have misunderstood who God is. You may have been raised to fear God and think of him as a far-off judge who is ready to knock you down for the slightest misbehavior. When you think of God, you may think of a harsh earthly father who is unkind, abusive, or distant. That's not what the Bible says God is like.

One of God's roles is judge. A time is coming when God will judge each and every one of us, but those of us who have trusted Jesus will have nothing to fear. God has already declared us not guilty! Because of Jesus' sacrifice on the cross for us, we can take heart, as we learn from these verses: "Therefore, there is now no condemnation for those who are in Christ Jesus, because through Christ Jesus the law of the Spirit who gives life has set you free from the law of sin and death" (Rom. 8:1–2). Instead of seeing God as judge, we can see him as our perfect heavenly Father.

When we accept Jesus, we are adopted into his family. He does this because he loves us. We are told in 1 John 3:1, "See what great love the Father has lavished on us, that we should be called children of God! And that is what we are!" We become part of God's family! Stop a second. Let that sink in. When you turn to Christ, you become part of God's family. That is huge! You'll never be alone again. You aren't an orphan. Even if you had terrible parents, you now have a perfect Father. When you admit you need God's power, you can trust him to give it to you. He is a good Father who wants to give you good gifts.

Jesus said to those who followed him, "If you, then, though you are evil, know how to give good gifts to your children, how much more will your Father in heaven give good gifts to those who ask him!" (Matt. 7:11). That part about "though you are evil" sounds harsh. But Jesus is pointing out that though we often have bad intentions, we can still give good gifts. God never has bad intentions, and he can't wait to give his children good gifts.

You can expect God to give you the grace, mercy, and power you need to overcome your problems. He is faithful.

He is good. He is kind. I've quoted many Bible verses in this section because I want you to see these qualities of God, but nothing will replace reading the Bible for yourself. You'll come to learn that God is willing and able to help you in your time of need. I love this verse from Hebrews: "Let us then approach God's throne of grace with confidence, so that we may receive mercy and find grace to help us in our time of need" (Heb. 4:16). If you are ready to seek help from God, remember that you can approach him with confidence and find the help you need.

Here's a quick word to those who do have a relationship with Jesus already: you might have a misconception about God too. Remind yourself of these Scriptures and never forget that God's grace and power are available to you, no matter what you may have done.

3. We're Afraid God Will Let Us Down

The third reason we don't turn to God for help is that we are afraid he won't come through. We need to make an important distinction here. God is not a genie. He will come through, but he might not do so in the way we hope. God doesn't do us the favor of conforming to our ideas about him or how he should work. Instead of solving our problem as we'd hoped he would, he might give us the power to get through it. God tends to work in ways we don't expect. The Bible says, "'For my thoughts are not your thoughts, neither are your ways my ways,' declares the LORD" (Isa. 55:8). There may be times when we want God to do a certain thing at a certain time, but he chooses to go another way. We have to remember that his ways aren't just different from ours; they are better than ours! We saw that God created the universe with a word. Someone with that kind of power can be trusted to help us in our problems, even when the solution doesn't look the way we thought it would.

Romans 8:28 says, "And we know that in all things God works for the good of those who love him, who have been called according to his purpose." There's another one of those "all things." That means he works out the good, the bad, and the ugly in your life for his purpose. It might not look like the solution you want, but it will work out for your good.

After you've admitted the problem to yourself and asked God for help, the next thing to do is attend a group. I'm going to admit something to you: I'm not really sure why support groups work. Talk about God working in a way that's different from mine. I honestly don't understand how sitting in a circle and sharing, without anyone trying to fix me, works so well. It isn't the solution I would have come up with. But I have learned that this process does work! There is power in sharing, and there is power in listening to others share. It might not feel natural, but it is so important. One thing I know is that you need other people to go through life with. You may find that you need a Celebrate Recovery group, a support group, or a counselor. Whatever you choose, fight against the temptation to isolate yourself. The Bible says, "Two are better than one, because they have a good return for their labor: If either of them falls down, one can help the other up. But pity anyone who falls and has no one to help them up. . . . Though one may be overpowered, two can defend themselves. A cord of three strands is not quickly broken" (Eccl. 4:9–10, 12). We all need other people.

When I was a kid at summer camp, the counselors always told us to stay with a buddy. If we needed to go to the bathroom, we were always supposed to go in pairs. There is safety in numbers. You will have times when you want to pull away and isolate yourself. You'll have times when going back to your old hurts, hang-ups, or habits seems better than this new way. Having a group of people around to keep you accountable is necessary for continued growth. Here's what I've learned from my experience: if you try to do it alone, you will fail! I wish I could be more optimistic about this, but I know from my experience and from watching others that those who try to do it alone, or even try to do it "just me and God," fail. Those who have a group of people around them to encourage and support them succeed.

God built this need for support into our lives. We see

it in James 5:16: "Therefore confess your sins to each other and pray for each other so that you may be healed. The prayer of a righteous person is powerful and effective." And in Hebrews 10:24–25: "And let us consider how we may spur one another on toward love and good deeds, not giving up meeting together, as some are in the habit of doing, but encouraging one another—and all the more as you see the Day approaching." And again in Acts 2:46: "Every day they continued to meet together in the temple courts. They broke bread in their homes and ate together with glad and sincere hearts." God wants us to be together in community.

Life Lesson 1 is this: Admitting you have problems doesn't make you weak; it makes you strong. It gives you the power you need from God, and it gives you the community and support you need from others. So if you find that you are one of *those* people, welcome. We aren't perfect; we are pretty messed up. But we are on the road to freedom, and we hope you'll join us.

Covering up problems always makes them worse

In Life Lesson 1, we explored how admitting we have problems isn't a weakness but a strength. But there's another side to that coin, Life Lesson 2: Covering up problems always makes them worse.

Life Lessons 1 and 2 are closely related, but they are also the opposite of each other. If admitting we have problems is a strength, then covering them up is a weakness. Worse than that, covering up our problems, trying to hide them from ourselves and others, or trying to pretend they don't even exist can make us feel like we have done something about them. Out of sight, out of mind. But if you've ever tried this, you know a covered-up problem is never out of mind.

This is how it always works for me. Something bad happens. I don't like it, so I pretend everything is okay. If it's my fault and I'm ashamed or embarrassed, I try to forget it. But other times it's something that has happened to me or just a bad situation. There's no one at fault; life happened. In any case, if I try to pretend it's all okay, that there's no problem, it always gets worse.

Leaks

We live in a leaky house. I'll bet you didn't know that is a thing, but our house is leak prone. We've lived in this little house in Southern California for more than ten years, and in those years we've had at least five leaks. We've had everything from toilets that flush on their own at 2:00 a.m., to hot-water heaters cracking at the bottom, to pinhole leaks in our walls, to a slab leak last summer. Jeni and I are at the point that when we hear a drip or running water, we panic. I've been known to walk around my house in the middle of the night with a flashlight searching for signs of leaks. I so wish this was a made-up story, but it's a hundred percent true. Just last night I jumped out of bed and ran to my back yard because I heard water running. It turned out to be a fountain my next-door neighbor had just installed. Jeni and

I may be the only people in the world who aren't relaxed by the sound of rainfall.

Last summer we had a slab leak. For months I had noticed the stucco on the side of our house got a little wet. I figured water was running from the sink, behind the cabinets, and down to the ground, but I told myself it was no big deal and that I'd deal with it when Jeni noticed. A few weeks later, I saw some moss growing on the wet spot on the wall. I thought, *That's pretty*, and moved on. About a month later, I got a call from my wife. "There's water running from our house into the neighbors' backyard!" I rushed home and called the plumber. Slab leak. Lots of money later, we had, instead of a summer vacation, beautiful new pipes you can't even see. Awesome.

I don't know for sure that if I had called a plumber at the first sign of a leak we would have avoided the cost of the repairs. But I do know that I could have avoided the anxiety and stress that the wet spot on the wall caused me every time I saw it. I could have avoided the late-night panic, worrying that we might wake up floating. I could have avoided the "discussion" Jeni and I had when she found out that I'd seen that spot months ago. Pretending the leak didn't exist didn't fix the leak. It made the damage worse and caused me stress. Pretending that our hurts, hang-ups, and habits don't exist does the same thing in our lives.

The book of Joshua has a powerful story about the cost

of covering up our problems. Right after the Israelites had taken the city of Jericho in an amazing victory, they experienced defeat. If you don't remember the story of the battle of Jericho, check it out in Joshua 6. The spoiler version is this: Jericho was a fortified city, with huge walls and gates that made it impossible for an army to attack. But God told Joshua he would conquer the city. All the Israelites had to do was walk around the walls of Jericho seven times, and on the seventh trip around, they were to shout and make a loud noise. When they did, the walls would come down so they could take the city. But God strictly warned them not to touch or take the things that were devoted to other gods, for fear they would distract the people from him.

Right after Jericho, there was another battle, this time with the town Ai. Whatever Jericho was, Ai wasn't. There weren't many people and the city was easy pickings. Some of Israel's military men came to Joshua and told him not to wear out the whole army by making them march and fight; a small force would suffice to take Ai. So Joshua sent about three thousand men to claim a decisive and easy victory.

But it wasn't a victory. The Israelites were beaten and embarrassed. They came running back, fell on their faces, cried, and asked God why he would allow such a thing to happen. I have this picture of God sighing heavily and telling Joshua, "Stand up! What are you doing down on your face? Israel has sinned; they have violated my covenant, which I commanded them to keep. They have taken some of the devoted things; they have stolen, they have lied, they have put them with their own possessions. That is why the Israelites cannot stand against their enemies; they turn their backs and run because they have been made liable to destruction. I will not be with you anymore unless you destroy whatever among you is devoted to destruction" (Josh. 7:10–12).

Whoa. Did you catch that? God told them he wouldn't be around them while they were not following him. So Joshua and the leaders went through the people of Israel and, tribe by tribe, family by family, sorted through everyone until they found the man responsible: Achan. Joshua asked Achan what he had done, and he responded that he had taken some of the devoted things. And, catch this part, "When I saw in the plunder a beautiful robe from Babylonia, two hundred shekels of silver and a bar of gold weighing fifty shekels, I coveted them and took them. They are hidden in the ground inside my tent, with the silver underneath" (Josh. 7:21). Achan knew what he had done was wrong, so he buried his treasure. He tried to hide it from his family, from his leaders, and from God.

This is so like us. Maybe you've never stolen devoted things, but I bet you've done something you weren't supposed to do and tried to hide it. I know I have. When I was active in my alcoholism, my wife and I lived in a small, two-bedroom condo. Since we didn't have kids yet, our second bedroom became our den with a sectional couch, a TV, and a computer desk. Eventually, and I still don't know how I managed this, it became sort of a man cave. We painted the walls a cranberry red, and the room took on a masculine feel.

Soon, Jeni stopped wanting to hang out in there, which was fine with me because I'd quickly thought of it as mine. I began drinking in there, usually when Jeni was either out or in bed, and I used the couch to hide my bottles. I stuffed them between the cushions. If you sat on that couch, it made a clinking sound when the bottles hit each other. It was a strange solution for a bar, but it worked because I could hide. I buried my treasure.

A friend of mine who struggles with sex addiction told me how he used to hide his browser history from his wife by making sure he deleted it every time he logged off. Whenever his wife went online, his heart beat fast, and he tried to get her to use a different computer. He was hiding his treasure.

Another friend told me how she used to hide her receipts and even opened a new credit card account to hide her purchases from her husband. I've heard people talk about leading separate lives, hiding huge portions of who they are from those closest to them. Many of us could tell our own stories. The thing that drove Achan to hide the devoted items, the thing that tells us to hide our secrets, our sins, our hurts, hang-ups, and habits, is this: we think we know better than God.

This goes back as far as it can, to the first couple, Adam and Eve. You know the story. Adam and Eve were given the entire garden of Eden, all of paradise, for their enjoyment. Except for one tree. One tree! They could eat anything except for the fruit of one tree. So what did they do? The same thing you and I would do: they ate the forbidden fruit. I don't know why this is true, but as soon as someone tells us not to do something, it's the only thing we want to do.

A while ago, my family and I were at Disneyland in line for the Indiana Jones ride. The line for that ride is long—really long—so they have built in all kinds of distractions to keep the people in line busy. There's a game to decipher a code, videos to watch, and all kinds of things to look at. At one point, there is a rope hanging from the ceiling going down into a well, and nearby an official sign says, "Do not pull rope! Handling fragile artifacts!" So what does everyone do? They pull the rope, eliciting a number of recorded responses, eventually ending with the "man on the rope" falling with a splash. The people at Disney understand human nature.

The Bible tells us that as soon as Adam and Eve did what they weren't supposed to do, their eyes were opened and they realized they were naked, so they made clothes to hide their nakedness. Then when God came walking in the garden, they tried to hide from him. But they couldn't hide from God, and we can't either. God had a plan for Adam and Eve, but they decided they knew better.

God has a plan for you and me, and often we decide we know better. But we don't. Whenever we do something we know we aren't supposed to and we try to cover it up, we are agreeing with God that we are wrong. People don't hide things they are proud of; they put them on display. We can get high and mighty with Adam and Eve and say, "If I'd been in their place, there's no way I would have eaten that fruit." But we all know we would have. We often know the right thing to do but don't do it, or we choose to do the wrong thing.

The apostle Paul knew this kind of thinking. In Romans 7 he writes, "I do not understand what I do. For what I want to do I do not do, but what I hate I do. And if I do what I do not want to do, I agree that the law is good. As it is, it is no longer I myself who do it, but it is sin living in me. For I know that good itself does not dwell in me, that is, in my sinful nature. For I have the desire to do what is good, but I cannot carry it out. For I do not do the good I want to do, but the evil I do not want to do—this I keep on doing" (Rom. 7:15–19). It's all right there. Like Paul, we often know the right thing to do, but we can't bring ourselves to do it. Meanwhile, the things we know we shouldn't do, we keep on doing. Listen, if the writer of half of the New Testament struggled with these issues, then it's silly for you and me to think we won't struggle with them.

I guess I should tell you how the story ended for Achan. After he was caught and admitted his sin, because he hadn't come forward on his own, Joshua was instructed by God to take Achan and his whole family outside the city gates and stone them. And then burn them.

Aren't you thankful for Jesus' sacrifice? Jesus paid the penalty for our sins on the cross. When we take our treasures and bury them in an attempt to hide them from God and other people, we are saying that we don't believe Christ's sacrifice was enough to cover us or our particular sin. We may have forgotten, or have never been told, that Christ paid the price for all of our sins.

But what if the thing we are covering isn't sin? What if it's a problem we don't want to face or a fear we want to push away? Covering those things makes them worse too. When we are tempted to cover something up, alarm bells should go off in our minds to warn us that we are in denial again.

Many of us were raised in families where we were not allowed to talk about certain issues. If that's your story, you can think of the forbidden topic that would ruin Thanksgiving if you brought it up at dinner. Pretending those things don't exist or trying to minimize them is covering them up, and when we do that, we allow them to have power over us. You may have heard the recovery cliché "you're only as sick as your secrets." That saying, like many in recovery, has become a cliché because it's true. Second Peter 2:19 says, "They promise them freedom, while they themselves are slaves of depravity—for 'people are slaves to whatever has mastered them.'" Our secrets become our masters.

It doesn't matter whether the thing we cover is our fault, something that was done to us, something we don't want to face, or simply something we have been told not to talk about, covering it makes it worse. Always. A bill has never been paid because someone was too afraid to open it and pay it. A tumor has never shrunk because a cancer patient decided not to get it looked at. The leak has never fixed itself, Johnny. And a sin or a habit has never lost power over anyone until they've had the courage to deal with it. The pain of the past or the fear of the future will forever lurk in the darkness until it is dragged out into the light of the truth.

Remember when I said I hate going to the dentist? Last summer, I put it off too long. Jeni and I were on a date night at our favorite Italian restaurant. I had a toothache that was so bad I could hear colors. I thought pasta would be a safe bet, but even chewing the noodles hurt my tooth. I asked for soup, but the heat was too much to handle. As I sat at the table dining on ibuprofen, Jeni informed me I was going to the dentist the next day. I went, and the doctor took some X-rays and sent me to an oral surgeon, who pulled two of my teeth.

You too may be trying to cover up a painful experience. Don't let it get worse.

What Should We Do?

So what should we do when we find that we have been covering up a problem?

First, if you need to, go back and reread the previous chapter. Remember that admitting you have a problem is the first step to healing, and it trades your limited power for God's ultimate power. Many of us who have been in recovery for a while will tell you that you may have to do this more than once. If you have been in recovery for a while, you may need to do this again right now.

You may have found some healing and victory over a particular hurt, hang-up, or habit but realized through a Step Study or conversation with your sponsor or accountability partner that you are covering up a different issue. If so, you may need to repeat the process of recovery for this issue. Don't worry, you don't lose all the hard work you've done so far; you will draw upon that work to start on this new issue and find new strength, freedom, and healing.

One of the tools we use in Celebrate Recovery are the workbooks written by Pastor John Baker called *The Journey Begins*. These four workbooks have helped millions of people on their recovery journey. When we go through these workbooks, we call it doing a Step Study. We get into gender-specific small groups and work, step-by-step, through the principles. Many people have gone through the Step Study once and found great help and victory over some hurts, hang-ups, and habits. Others have decided to work through the workbooks more than once because they uncovered a new area that needed attention. They decided to dig deeper and keep uncovering hurt in their lives. That's why Pastor John and I wrote the follow-up workbooks called *The Journey Continues* to help people go even farther on their recovery journey.

Going through multiple Step Studies isn't starting over; it's going farther.

If you're new to recovery or if you're still not sure recovery applies to you, and you have not yet admitted you have problems, start there. But then do something about it. Just like I can say it's time to hit the gym because I'm out of shape, until I clean up my diet and start working out, nothing changes. Covering up our problems is like finding a baggy shirt to wear instead of going to the gym. I've admitted I'm out of shape, and I've found a solution that makes me feel better, but still nothing has changed. Don't get stuck in this cycle. When you admit you have a problem, fight the inner voice that tells you to take a break and not do the next needed thing.

I've seen this happen time and time again. Someone comes to Celebrate Recovery and admits that their hurts, hang-ups, or habits are out of control, and they feel relief. All of a sudden, that closely guarded secret loses its power. I can see their shoulders rise as if a burden has been lifted from them. They experience what Jesus was talking about when he said, "Come to me, all you who are weary and burdened, and I will give you rest. Take my yoke upon you and learn from me, for I am gentle and humble in heart, and you will find rest for your souls. For my yoke is easy and my burden is light" (Matt. 11:28–30). When we turn to Jesus, he lifts our burdens. That's why we feel better even though nothing has really changed yet. But that feeling of relief can trap us because we miss what Jesus says in the second part of that verse, when he tells us to take his yoke in exchange for our burdens. According to the dictionary, a yoke is "a bar or frame that is attached to the heads or necks of two work animals (such as oxen) so that they can pull a plow or heavy load." When Jesus tells us to take up his yoke, it means we have some work to do.

Following Jesus is full of verbs. We don't come to him and find rest and take a nap. It's a different kind of rest. Rest from anxiety, rest from trying to pretend we have it all together, rest from the effort it takes to try to live on our own power, but not rest from work. Recovery is work, but we have a loving, gentle, and humble leader who is driving us on the journey. He tells us that he won't burden us with unnecessary things; we can find a new way of living. We find rest when we come to Jesus, take up his yoke, and, with his guidance and power and with the other people yoked to us, head down the road to recovery.

Once we experience relief or rest, we have to work on the issues that come up. If the problem has a simple solution, like a bill or a leak or a brake job or a toothache, it's as simple as facing the truth, as scary as it may be, and then doing what needs to be done. Like calling the company we owe money to and working out a payment plan, or calling a plumber to come and take a look, or getting the car to the shop, or going to the dentist. It might not be fun, but the resulting sense of accomplishment turns into momentum that makes tackling problems a lot easier. Soon you'll learn to turn problems into opportunities.

What if it's a stickier situation? What if it's a habit that you have tried to break or the pain someone has caused you? What if it isn't as easy as just dealing with it? Then I would suggest a step-by-step process. Twelve steps. Give Celebrate Recovery a try, and work the steps and principles as so many have before you. Don't be like Achan; be like Paul.

Even though Paul struggled with his sin, he knew that Jesus was there for him and that he would make him right. After lamenting his inability to do the right thing, he writes, "What a wretched man I am! Who will rescue me from this body that is subject to death? Thanks be to God, who delivers me through Jesus Christ our Lord!" (Rom. 7:24–25). Instead of covering up his struggles, he recorded them in his letters so that those who read them, including us thousands of years later, would be encouraged to do the same and to find the answer he found.

Who can help us? Jesus can. There's no need to cover up our problems, because God has delivered us through Jesus. Jesus will give us the rest we need and the guidance to move in a better direction, and he will bring us together with other people who are experiencing the same need. That's a pretty great trade. Covering up our problems always makes them worse. Turning them over to Jesus always makes them better.

Small, steady improvement lasts longer than overnight change

About four years ago, my brother-in-law invited me to train for a half marathon with him. For some reason, he thought it would be fun to do together. I have a great relationship with him and enjoy spending time with him, so I said yes. He sent me a training spreadsheet to help me get ready for the race. I'm not a runner. Until he sent me the spreadsheet, the last mile I had run was in high school. But I was a little out of shape and thought I needed a goal, so I signed up.

The training was laid out, week to week, to get us ready to run the thirteen miles in a few months. It was simple and straightforward. The first week, we were to run one mile on two different days. That was it. I looked at that and thought, *Well, this will be easy.* I set out to run the first mile, and while it was hard, I got it done in under twelve minutes. I bristled at the idea that only twelve minutes would be the entire workout.

The second day I ran the mile again and decided that this plan was really for people who were severely out of shape. People like me, who were only mildly out of shape, could adjust the regimen. So I added miles to the plan. If the plan said run a mile, I ran two. After all, if one is good, two is better. If it said two, I ran three. When it said four, I decided I wouldn't lace up my very new, very expensive running shoes for less than five.

Along with the new shoes, I bought a backpack that has a built-in water bottle so I wouldn't have to carry a bottle in my hands. I also bought GU packets: a sugar paste that runners eat while they run to give them carbohydrates and electrolytes. I visited runner's websites and bought running magazines. I began to eat like a runner. I wanted to get lighter so I could increase my speed. When work or life got in the way of my run, I got crabby and complained.

I pushed myself to run longer and faster. One Saturday, my wife wanted to go to a farmers' market. I told her I would run and meet her there. It was nine miles from my door to the market. I knew I wouldn't be able to run home, so my plan was to run there and then go home with her and the kids. The spreadsheet was a distant memory. I felt bad for the suckers who had to follow it. It wasn't a plan for *real* runners.

I set out on the path. About five miles in, my left knee began to hurt. I needed to run through the pain, that's what all the articles I had read said. The experts said to ignore the pain. So I did. The pain grew worse as the run went on, but I pushed through. About a quarter of a mile from the market, I had to stop for the first time. The running path had ended, and I was on the regular sidewalk and at a crosswalk. As I waited, I did the thing that runners do while they wait for the light to change: I jogged in place and took my pulse. I tried to ignore the intensifying pain. I was almost there. I stopped for a moment to stretch, and the signal changed for me to cross the street.

Then it happened. As I stepped off the curb into the street, my left leg buckled, then locked up. When I stepped on my right foot, pain shot up from the ball of my foot to the top of my head. I did a two-legged limping movement that probably would have been funny if it hadn't hurt so badly. For the rest of the quarter mile, I limped along until I got to Jeni. She took one look at me and knew I was in bad shape. She said, "Looks like you're going to the doctor." I told her it would be okay. I would drink some water and shake it off.

About an hour later, I was on the phone with a sports medicine doctor making an appointment. When I went in to see the doctor, I told him about my "plan" and that I had run 120 miles in six weeks. He looked at me like he didn't comprehend what I said. He asked how many miles I had run leading up to those six weeks, and I sheepishly said, "Zero?" I noticed that didn't clear up the look of confusion, so I said, "Maybe I should tell you I'm a recovering alcoholic." He looked at me, crumpled up the notes on his clipboard, and said, "We have to start all the way over with you."

He told me the race was off. I had hurt my left IT band and bruised a bone in my right foot. I needed at least three to six weeks of rest to heal. Once that was over, he said, I could start running again, but I'd have to limp into it and actually follow a training program. He assured me I would run again. I left his office and iced my knee and dreamed about the day I'd get to run again. A few weeks later, I got the all-clear, laced up my shoes, ran out my front door, and stopped a hundred feet down the sidewalk. I remembered that I hate running. The madness was over. I haven't run a mile since.

Imagine what would have happened had I followed the program as it was laid out. I would have progressed much more slowly. Instead of running 120 miles in six weeks, I might have run only twenty miles. I might not have been able to brag about how far I was running, but I would have been able to run a much farther distance in the long term. What if instead of running 120 miles in six weeks I instead ran ten miles a week for the last four years? At fifty-two weeks a year, that's 208 weeks and a total of 2,080 miles. Now, I'm not good at math (if you think I didn't use a calculator to come up with those figures, you're dreaming), but 2,080 is just a little farther than 120. Instead of a six-week obsession, I could have developed a lifelong healthy habit. My heart would be in better shape and so would my body.

The third thing I have come to learn about life from Celebrate Recovery is this: small steady improvement lasts longer than overnight change. This kind of change isn't what most of us want, but it's what lasts. Many come to Celebrate Recovery looking for instant, complete change. We want to show up for the first time, admit we have a problem, maybe say a prayer, and find deliverance. But that isn't what most of us find.

To those of you who have had that instant deliverance, I want to say I think it's awesome! I'm so excited that God did that for you. If you prayed and found your compulsion was lifted, I think that is amazing.

But I have often found that those who have had that experience miss this truth: they have left pain in their wake. Many miss the opportunity to work out their recovery journey because they feel like they are better or cured.

If this is your experience, you need to understand that the people around you who were affected by your issues did not have the same instant healing that you did, and they might still have pain in their lives that is a consequence of your actions. Telling them that you are different now may not be enough for them. They would benefit from your working a program. Also, all of us have more than one issue that we could apply the recovery principles to.

I prayed for years that my desire to drink would just go away, but my compulsion to act out with alcohol needed help in the form of Celebrate Recovery. Now I pray for God to take away my anxiety. Just last week I woke up with such bad anxiety I couldn't go back to sleep. Thanks to God and Celebrate Recovery, I haven't had a drink in more than twelve years, but I still have issues, including anxiety, that I still need to apply the principles of recovery to every day. No matter how we find the healing we are looking for, whether it comes in a flash or takes one day at a time, it all comes from God.

God Isn't Done with You Yet!

If you are new to Celebrate Recovery or if you have been working the program for a short time and you don't feel like you are where you should be yet, I have good news for you: God isn't done with you yet!

Philippians 1:6 says, "He who began a good work in you will carry it on to completion until the day of Christ Jesus."

"He who began a good work." It is God who begins the good work in us. It might feel like we are the ones beginning the work by coming out of denial and admitting we have a problem, but the stirring to take that step comes from God. There are two jobs: God's job and mine. When it comes to recovery, there are things I have to do, and there are things only God can do. God prompts us to take the steps; he begins the work. We follow him and take the steps he directs for us.

"Will carry it on to completion." The verse doesn't say, "He who began a good work in you completed it," does it? No! It says "will carry it on to completion." That's such an important distinction because it reminds me that I'm not done yet. From time to time, someone will ask me how long I think they are going to have to be in recovery. I always tell them the same thing: "I don't know how long for you. I know this for sure, though: I'm not done yet." God is still working things out in my life. There are issues I need to face, things I need to deal with, hurts, hang-ups, and habits, or what we sometimes refer to as character defects, in my life that are unresolved. God isn't done with me yet.

We are told, "For it is by grace you have been saved, through faith—and this is not from yourselves, it is the gift of God—not by works, so that no one can boast. For we are

God's handiwork, created in Christ Jesus to do good works, which God prepared in advance for us to do" (Eph. 2:8–10). Our salvation is a gift of God, and we can't earn it. He gives it to us freely. He begins the work in us, but we also find that we were made to do good works. When we understand that God began this work in us, it should give us confidence and strength to follow through. We don't have to maintain the strength to keep going, because God has given us the strength from the start.

In my last Step Study, I didn't focus on or share about my struggle with alcohol. Not once. Why? Because I have been sober for more than a decade. Now, I still identify as "Johnny, a believer who struggles with alcoholism," because the minute I think my struggle is over, I have set myself up for a relapse. But I don't have to fight the temptation to drink from day to day. However, I do still struggle with codependency.

Many people define codependency in many ways. If you were to poll a hundred codependents and ask them to define the term, you would most likely get a hundred different definitions. But I'm writing this, so I'll tell you mine. In my life, codependency looks an awful lot like people pleasing. I told you there were some leaders and participants in our Celebrate Recovery group at Saddleback who resented my involvement, believing I was hired because I was Pastor John's son. They weren't shy about letting me know it either. I would leave our Friday night meetings in turmoil as I began to believe that maybe I shouldn't be there. I was allowing my critics to determine my effectiveness. I wanted them all to like me. Some of them came around, and I count them as my dear friends and partners in ministry. Some left.

The people pleaser in me wanted to chase them and tell them why they were wrong, or even worse, wanted to conform to their picture of who I should be. Thankfully, I have a few great mentors who helped me see that even if I changed everything about me, I would never be able to change the thing they resented. I'd still be Pastor John's son. Talk about something I wouldn't want to change! But this people-pleasing tendency, this codependency, is a struggle for me today.

So when I am tempted to look at my years of sobriety from alcohol and think, *I've come a long way, baby,* I remember that I have about thirty seconds of sobriety from people pleasing. But that doesn't discourage or distract me. Why? Because God isn't done with me yet! I can boldly proclaim that I have issues and brag about being a mess. One of the key verses of Celebrate Recovery is, "But he said to me, 'My grace is sufficient for you, for my power is made perfect in weakness.' Therefore I will boast all the more gladly about my weaknesses, so that Christ's power may rest on me" (2 Cor. 12:9). We, like Paul, have found that since God isn't done with us yet, it means his power is still available to us. God isn't done with me yet, and he isn't done with you either.

"Until the day of Christ Jesus." When will God be done with us? Only when Jesus returns or he takes us home to heaven. Look around you. He hasn't come back yet, and if you're reading this, he hasn't taken you home yet. That's how we can know—not guess but know—that God isn't done with us.

One day, his work in us will be complete. One day, we will see Jesus and know the meaning of the words, "For now we see only a reflection as in a mirror; then we shall see face to face. Now I know in part; then I shall know fully, even as I am fully known" (1 Cor. 13:12). In that moment, we will be without sin, without pain, without tears. We will be made perfect. Until then, we will struggle, we will sin, but we will also have hope.

Christ is making us better one day at a time. The storms of life will come. Remember what happened when Jesus and his disciples were in the middle of a storm. When the disciples began to panic that the storm would sink their boat, "He [Jesus] got up, rebuked the wind and said to the waves, 'Quiet! Be still!' Then the wind died down and it was completely calm. He said to his disciples, 'Why are you so afraid? Do you still have no faith?' They were terrified and asked each other, 'Who is this? Even the wind and the waves obey him!'" (Mark 4:39–41). You have the power of Christ. You will not sink!

We are looking for steady improvement, not immediate perfection. Steady improvement is sustainable, and steady improvement is actual change.

Steady Improvement Is Sustainable

When I trained for a half marathon, I tried to go from zero to 120. I blew out my knee and bruised a bone in my foot. After I healed up, I never ran again. My pace was not sustainable.

When I began recovery, I was working as a manager in a chain restaurant. Since I was the newest manager, I worked many late nights doing paperwork and accounting while the kitchen staff cleaned up from the busy dinner shift. I spent some of those late nights in the office reading recovery material and Christian books.

One day, my friend, a pastor at Saddleback, came over and saw my stack of books. He asked me about them, and I told him about my voracious reading appetite. He said, "Look, I don't know too much about recovery, but I know this: you are sprinting and you're going to wear yourself out. Pace yourself." He was one of the people I had turned to when I was trying to talk myself out of following God's call to enter ministry. He gave me immediate encouragement and followed up with emails and phone calls asking me if

I had signed up for seminary. He told me about potential job openings at Saddleback. Now here he was telling me to slow down! Luckily, I had already learned to listen to his wisdom, and we talked about sustainable growth. I did slow down, but I didn't stop.

When we set unrealistic expectations of ourselves, in recovery or any area of our lives, we are setting ourselves up for disappointment. Pastor Rick Warren says, "We overestimate what we can achieve with a short-term goal, and we underestimate what we can achieve with a long-term goal."

Often people come to Celebrate Recovery with a list of hurts, hang-ups, or habits they want to change. They jump into recovery with both feet and try to attend every group they can. While I recommend attending as many meetings as one feels he or she needs, I don't think jumping from issue group to issue group is a good idea. We need to focus on one issue at a time. If you begin recovery looking for sobriety in chemical dependency, don't also work on your anger issues, codependency, and spending habits. If you begin recovery to work on love and relationship issues, don't also focus on food issues and quitting smoking. Why? Because we need to focus on one issue at a time. We always recommend that people begin with the issue that is causing them the most pain right now. It doesn't mean that there won't be time to work on those other issues, but we need to do them one at a time.

There's an adage in recovery: "How do you eat an elephant? One bite at a time." How do you find healing for the variety of hurts, hang-ups, or habits in your life? One day at a time, one issue at a time. The timing of each of these can vary. I don't focus daily on my struggle with alcohol anymore, but every day is a battle for sobriety in codependency. Focusing on one issue at a time makes the changes sustainable. This is true in recovery, dieting, marathon training, and any other endeavor we wish to find lasting success in. Trying to do too much too soon is a surefire way to fail. Focusing on steady improvement is maintainable and sustainable and allows us to add to each small victory.

Steady Improvement Is Actual Change

I spent five years in the community-college system. I say it like that because I hope some people might be tricked into thinking I was a professor. I wasn't; I was a student. Well, I attended classes sometimes, if I felt like it. I mastered the art of dropping a class when I could get a W, which meant I withdrew from the class before grades counted instead of outright failing. I did eventually finish college and got a degree.

The beginning of every semester at my community college was the same. The parking lot would be so full, students would arrive hours before class to get a spot. The ultra-expensive required books were sold out weeks before the class began. Once we arrived to class, the seats would all be full and some students had to stand, because so many people were auditing the class, trying to add it to their schedule.

As the weeks went by, things changed. The parking lot became less crowded and some premium spots opened up. The bookstore had discounted books for sale, and the classrooms had plenty of seats. People like me dropped the classes. Our intentions were good, but we didn't follow through.

Every semester, I'd tell myself, and my mom, that this time I finally had it together. I would not only sign up for school, but I'd actually study! I'd get good grades—no, I'd get straight A's! This was my time. I would sign up, show up, and will myself to become a student. Then the work would get hard or I'd get distracted, and I'd miss an assignment. The spiral would begin. One missed assignment would become a pattern, and I'd eventually get so behind, I would be buried by the workload and by the shame, so I'd drop out. Repeat, repeat, repeat. It wasn't until I met Jeni that I got serious about school. I wanted to marry her so badly, and I wanted to deserve her, so I followed through on my commitments. It didn't hurt that I found a school that worked well with my learning style, that had a different pace and teaching style.

I wanted to be a good student, I wanted to graduate, I wanted to change, but because I tried to do too much too soon, I failed over and over. Have you ever decided this was the time to get fit and head to the gym and do every exercise in the place? Just me? If you have, you know that two things happen: you wake up the next morning sore, and you don't go back to the gym. One workout won't give us defined abs, just like one run won't make us a marathoner, just like one class won't make us a scholar, just like one recovery meeting won't make us sober. Real change takes time.

To find the change we are looking for, we need to realize it won't be quick. It might even be hard, but it will be worth it. If you can understand that, then no matter what you are trying to change, you will avoid disappointment, frustration, and burnout.

I am not the man I hope someday to become. I am much better than I used to be, but I have a long way to go.

I love the words of Paul in Philippians 3: "Not that I have already obtained all this, or have already arrived at my goal, but I press on to take hold of that for which Christ Jesus took hold of me. Brothers and sisters, I do not consider myself yet to have taken hold of it. But one thing I do: Forgetting what is behind and straining toward what is ahead, I press on toward the goal to win the prize for which God has called me heavenward in Christ Jesus" (Phil. 3:12–14). The day-by-day change that Christ offers as he pulls us toward himself is life change. It's long lasting. It won't happen overnight, it might even be so small and slow moving that we hardly notice, but the change we find will be sustainable and real.

How Do We Apply This to Life?

Set reasonable goals.

This is the most important and hardest step. Look at where you hope to be a year from now and set weekly or monthly goals for how you will arrive there. Be aware that the actual growth may be different than you are expecting. The journey you go on may not be the one you set out on, but if you give yourself goals, you will eventually reach the destination.

Look at a big goal and break it down into parts. Ask yourself how you'll get there and then map it out.

- I want to achieve a year of sobriety.
  - How will I get there?
  - What are my daily and monthly goals?
  - What will I do when I get discouraged or triggered to act out?
- I want to save money.
  - What is my budget plan?
  - What am I saving for?
  - Will I be able to live on the budget I'm planning, or is it too strict?
- I want to get physically healthy.
  - What diet or workout plan will I follow?
  - What does healthy mean? Losing weight, running a marathon, becoming active?

⊚ How can I break it down into smaller, measurable goals?

These are just three examples; there are many more. The point is to look at a big goal and break it down into parts. Ask yourself how you'll get there and then map it out. Remember the words of Pastor Rick Warren: "We overestimate what we can achieve with a short-term goal, and we underestimate what we can achieve with a long-term goal." If we add up lots of reasonable, reachable, short-term goals, we can look back over a long term and find we have achieved incredible growth and results. One day at a time.

The most powerful tool anyone has in his or her toolbox in this area of achieving small, progressive growth is to ask for input from others. Other people can see the small changes in us faster than we can see them ourselves. Sharing your goals enables people to hold you accountable and to point out times when they see the changes in you.

Celebrate the Small Changes

It doesn't matter what the change is. When you realize you've changed, celebrate it. If you're driving on the freeway and get cut off and you wave with all five fingers instead of one, celebrate that change! When you find yourself in a situation that would have brought you anxiety and you find that you are trusting God, celebrate it. If you enjoy one day of sobriety, celebrate it. Celebrate the salad you ordered instead of the triple cheeseburger. Change that we do not enjoy will not last. Change we celebrate, even the smallest change, will grow into long-lasting life change.

As we apply this Life Lesson, we will see that no matter the area of growth, no matter the hurt, hang-up, or habit, growth and change can happen. The goal is to stop looking for overnight change and instead ask God to give us steady, day-by-day growth. This kind of growth is real and sustainable and over time leads to amazing life change.

And never forget, God isn't finished with you yet!

Pain has purpose

Have you ever had something uncomfortable to do, so you just put it off? I have. Like, every day. The other day, I had some important paperwork I needed to sign and mail off. I knew I needed to do it, but for some reason, I put it off. I lay awake at night and thought about that stack of papers. I told myself I would wake up, sign them, and rush off to overnight them. Then I woke up and put it off.

I guess there was something about signing my name that made me nervous, because signing my name was all that was required of me. The paperwork wasn't scary, I didn't do anything wrong, I wasn't in trouble, but I was going to be if I didn't send it in. One morning, I kept my promise. I signed it and sent it in. I survived.

Still another time I needed to send an email to someone to ask for help. I drafted the email and then deleted it. Then I wrote it and deleted it again. I did this over and over. Finally, I sent the email. I survived.

Fear is a kind of pain, and pain can be a great paralyzer. But it can also be a great motivator. I'm afraid of going to the dentist, but pain gets me in that seat. Pain is uncomfortable, and most of us would be just fine avoiding pain for the rest of our lives. But here's the truth: pain has a purpose.

You and I have been lied to, and many of us have believed that lie. The lie is that pain is useless and that people who have been through great pain are useless. We have been told by people, by ourselves, and by the enemy that if we have gone through pain, we are broken. We have been told that broken people have no value. You may have been told that God can't use you, not after what you've done or what's been done to you. If you have believed that lie, you may think that you'll never be good enough for God. You may believe that you'll never be used by him to help others. If that's how you feel, I have great news for you. Not only can God use broken people to serve him and help others; broken people are the only ones he uses.

In the Bible, God uses broken men and women to serve him and help other people. It's easy to elevate the people in the Bible and think that God could use them because they were special or because they somehow impressed God so much he couldn't help but use them. But with the exception of Jesus, every man and woman we read about in the Bible is a flawed individual with hurts, hang-ups, and habits. Pick someone in the Bible. Read their story. You'll see that God used their pain and weakness as much as he used their strength.

There is a whole chapter in the Bible that many have called the Hall of Faith. In Hebrews 11 we are given a list of the people who served God in amazing ways. They are the all-stars, the people we all look up to. There's Abraham, Issac, Jacob, Joseph, Rahab, and more. They are heroes, but they are all deeply flawed. Abraham lied when it was convenient for him. Jacob deceived his father. Joseph provoked his brothers' envy. Rahab was a prostitute. This group of people was special not because of who they were but because they had faith. It's that simple.

They had faith in God. He used them not in spite of their weaknesses but through them. I would be so bold as to say that God uses only broken people. Don't believe me? Check it out yourself. Go through the Bible and try to find one man or woman who had it all together. You won't find anyone. God uses broken people.

Everyone who has ever been used by God has experienced pain. That means you and me, but it also means your pastor. It means your sponsor or the people you look up to. It means the missionary who is winning souls in Africa, and it means the person in the pew next to you who tries to make it look like he or she has it all together. If God is using someone, it means that they have gone through pain.

The apostle Paul is arguably the most influential Christ follower in history. He wrote a huge portion of the New Testament, and his words have been encouraging, challenging, and correcting Christians for generations. I love reading Paul's writings because his honesty about himself is so refreshing. Paul was used by Jesus in mighty ways, yet he knew pain.

Paul's Thorn

In one of his letters, Paul tells the church in Corinth, "Therefore, in order to keep me from becoming conceited, I was given a thorn in my flesh, a messenger of Satan, to torment me. Three times I pleaded with the Lord to take it away from me" (2 Cor. 12:7–8). I don't know whether this thorn was physical or spiritual, but I know it was painful. Paul was tormented by it. This was in addition to all of the whippings, shipwrecks, and imprisonment he endured for the sake of Christ. Paul was used by God in great ways, and he went through great pain.

He said this after he pleaded with Jesus to take away this thorn: "But he [Jesus] said to me, 'My grace is sufficient for you, for my power is made perfect in weakness.' Therefore

I will boast all the more gladly about my weaknesses, so that Christ's power may rest on me. That is why, for Christ's sake, I delight in weaknesses, in insults, in hardships, in persecutions, in difficulties. For when I am weak, then I am strong" (2 Cor. 12:9–10). Like all believers, even the ones we place on a pedestal and wish we could be more like, Paul went through pain, and God used his pain to help others.

All broken people who have been used by God acknowledge their pain and brokenness. This is essential to recovery—it's the first of the eight principles—but it is necessary for anyone who hopes to be used by God. As long as we think we are serving God from our own strength, we won't be leaning on him for his power. We must admit we have pain and brokenness. Paul didn't just admit he had weaknesses, but he boasted about them!

That's something we do in Celebrate Recovery when we share with others our hurts, hang-ups, and habits. We are boasting about our weaknesses, our pain, our struggles. In doing so, we are being used by God to help others. You may not be aware of this, but if you have ever shared during a Celebrate Recovery meeting, you have been used by God to help someone else.

Even if you shared only a struggle, even if you shared only your pain, even if you shared only your brokenness, you have helped someone else. You have comforted or encouraged the people in your circle with your sharing. You have shown others that it is safe for them to share because of your courage in sharing. You are a part of a huge tradition of finding comfort and then passing that comfort on.

People who are used by God have gone through and acknowledged their pain. But why must we go through any pain at all? We go through pain because pain has a purpose. Pain is a great motivator. Pain gets us moving. As I sit here writing this, I find myself in a painful situation. It's my jeans; they are too tight. For the last few months I have put my physical health on the back burner while I've been writing this book and focusing on some important things at Celebrate Recovery. Here's something you should know about me: I enjoy working out. Most of the time. I like the physical release it offers me and enjoy the time in the gym. But I have found out that it is really easy to break a good habit. So now I sit here typing and I'm uncomfortable in my jeans. I'm tempted to think they shrank in the wash, but I know the truth: I've been neglecting my physical health. I've been eating what I want, when I want, and I haven't been working out. I'm no genius, but that's not a great combination. The "pain" of tight jeans—I might be overstating things a bit, but stay with me— has gotten my attention. It's time to do something about it. Now, as with all different kinds of pain, I have a choice. The choice I have about my physical health is the same choice we have when it comes to our spiritual health: I can either do something about it or pretend it's all okay.

In my example, doing something about it would be cleaning up my diet and getting back to working out. Pretending it's okay would be going to the mall and buying larger jeans, blaming my tight jeans on the dryer, or ignoring the problem altogether. Pain is the motivator. For me, I'll soon be taking a break from the writing and get to the gym.

When it comes to real pain, we have an important choice: we can either draw near to God, or we can run away from him. This is especially true if the pain we are going through is because of our own doing, what we would call sin, but it is also true of pain we go through because of circumstances outside of our control. One of the functions of pain in our lives is to turn us back to, or get us closer to, our loving Father. One of my favorite stories in the Bible is Jesus' parable of the Prodigal Son (Luke 15). It is such a great example of how pain can be used to draw us to God, and what we can find in God when we come to him.

The Prodigal Son

A rich man has two sons. One of his sons comes to him and asks for his inheritance. He doesn't want to wait for his father to die before he receives his share of the family's wealth. He wants to enjoy it now. Because his father loves him, he gives him the money, and the son heads off to the biblical equivalent of Las Vegas, where he blows all his money on parties and women. For a brief time, he has it all. But as soon as the money runs out, he finds himself alone and destitute and needing to work. He winds up taking a job feeding pigs, and he is so hungry he wishes he could eat what the pigs are eating.

One day, he comes to his senses. "I should just go home," he thinks. He knows he can't return to his place as his father's son, but he figures his father's servants are treated better than he is being treated now. So he decides to go home. On the way he practices his speech. He says, "I will set out and go back to my father and say to him: Father, I have sinned against heaven and against you. I am no longer worthy to be called your son; make me like one of your hired servants" (Luke 15:18–19). I love this image of him walking and practicing his speech; I can see him imagining all kinds of scenarios. Will his father throw him out? Will he take him in as a servant but punish him? Will he pretend he doesn't know him? But he keeps walking. The pain has motivated him to turn back to his father.

Jesus goes on to say that when the son is still far away from the house, the father sees him and begins to run toward him. I love this part of the story because it tells us so much about our Father, God. The father in the story sees the son coming and runs toward him. The father was looking for his son. He was anticipating his arrival.

So the father runs to his son and hugs him. The son breaks into his speech about not being good enough to be called a son, and I can see the father laughing and crying and calling to his servants, "'Quick! Bring the best robe and put it on him. Put a ring on his finger and sandals on his feet. Bring the fattened calf and kill it. Let's have a feast and celebrate. For this son of mine was dead and is alive again; he was lost and is found.' So they began to celebrate" (Luke 15:22–24). The father is ready to forgive and love his son because he loves him so much. He puts the mark of sonship on him—the ring—and accepts him back into the family. He doesn't make him sweat it out; he doesn't punish him first. He just takes him back in as his son.

Jesus told this story to illustrate what God is like. So often we go against what God has for us. We think we know what's best for us and we go our own way. That always leads to pain. When we find ourselves in pain and out of God's will, we have the choice the Prodigal Son had. We can wallow in our pain, or we can run back to our Father. When we do, we don't find a Father waiting to punish us; we don't find a Father waiting for us to say the right things or earn our place as his child again. We find a loving and forgiving Father who celebrates our coming home.

One important purpose of pain is to draw us near to God. It is my belief that God allows us to go through pain as a way to get our attention. He will allow the pain to increase until we turn our hearts to him. If you are going through pain right now, whether it's your doing or not, ask yourself if it's time to return to God. Lamentation 3:40 says, "Let us examine our ways and test them, and let us return to the Lord." If you find that you have a sin in your life that is causing you or others pain, take the example of the Prodigal Son and return to Jesus. When you do you will find acceptance and forgiveness. You'll also be able to use your story as a way to help other people. When you share with them how you turned from your sin and ran to God, you'll be able to help them do the same thing.

Pain's Second Purpose

Because that's the second purpose of pain, to help us serve other people. If Celebrate Recovery has a theme verse, it would probably be 2 Corinthians 1:3–4, "Praise be to the God and Father of our Lord Jesus Christ, the Father of compassion and the God of all comfort, who comforts us in all our troubles, so that we can comfort those in any trouble with the comfort we ourselves receive from God." I love this verse. It says so much about how Celebrate Recovery works. We come to Celebrate Recovery in our pain and we find comfort from someone else, then we are used by God to pass that comfort on to someone else. Isn't that amazing?

Pain provides us two choices: where will we go with

our pain, and what will we do with our pain? Will you allow your pain to draw you nearer to God or to push you away from him? Will you use your pain to help others, or will you allow it to isolate you from others? When faced with a painful situation, what will you do with your pain? Let's be honest, no matter how good life is today, a painful experience is ahead of us. I don't say that to be depressing or as a fatalist, but as a warning and as a realist. We cannot hide our heads in the sand and pretend that life is going to be carefree forever.

A few months ago my family and I were having a great day. We went to the beach, then later in the afternoon, my wife took my kids to the park to play with friends. My middle child, Chloe, was heading down a hill on a scooter when she took a nasty fall and hit her head. (She wasn't wearing a helmet.) Jeni called me and I could hear the worry in her voice. Chloe didn't pass out, but a hit to the head is scary. She also had a big gash in her side. We were honestly more worried about the cut, so we decided to go to the ER just in case. While we were there they checked her head injury and decided to order a CT scan. Then our world crashed in.

They said they thought they saw bleeding on her brain. Chloe was rushed to the trauma room and had nurses and doctors all around her. Chloe was understandably shaken and panicked. So were we. After about an hour there they decided she should stay in the Pediatrics Intensive Care Unit for the night. When we got up there the nurses and doctors were so much calmer. They explained that the pediatrician in that PICU wing and a neurologist both agreed that there was no bleeding; they didn't even think she had a concussion! They said Chloe was far too responsive and that the "bleeding" they saw on the CT scan was too unclear to think there was a problem. Even the radiologist said she thought it was probably due to a slight movement during the test. They kept Chloe overnight but relaxed the concussion protocol, and by morning she was released.

In a matter of hours we went from an ideal family day to one of the scariest nights of our lives. Pain came crashing in when we least expected it. We had the best possible result, yet we were shaken. After writing this I had to stop for a minute and call my wife so she could put Chloe on the phone, just so I could hear her voice and reassure myself that she was okay. The pain still lingers. Pain is inevitable, but what we do with that pain is up to us.

Your pain may look very different from mine. Your painful situation may take the form of someone finding out about a hidden addiction or behavior. It may be relational pain, when someone in your life mistreats you or hurts you. You may have relapsed and gone back to an old hurt, hang-up, or habit. It might take the form of a job loss or a parent passing or any number of things.

What Will You Do with Your Pain?

The important question is: what choice will you make with your pain? Will you allow it to push you away from God, or will you draw nearer to him? We are told in the book of James, "Come near to God and he will come near to you" (James 4:8). When we come closer to God, he comes closer to us. Remember, God will use our pain to get our attention. C. S. Lewis said, "We can ignore even pleasure. But pain insists upon being attended to. God whispers to us in our pleasures, speaks in our conscience, but shouts in our pains: it is his megaphone to rouse a deaf world." The Bible says it this way, "And we know that in all things God works for the good of those who love him, who have been called according to his purpose" (Rom. 8:28).

There are two important things to point out about this verse. First, God uses *all* things for our good. Not *some* things, not the good things, not our successes, but *all* things. Big and small. Positive and negative. Wins and losses. The things we want to post on social media and the things we want to hide. He uses *all* things for our good! That includes your pain!

The second thing to point out is that while God uses all things for our good, he doesn't cause all things to happen. We, and others, have free will. That means we choose to do the wrong thing sometimes. That's called sin, and sin has consequences. One consequence of sin is pain. Pain for us and pain for those around us. God does not cause us or others to sin. But he allows us to choose sin, and then, if we let him, he uses the pain of sin for our good.

How do we let God work? In the two ways we have already discussed! First, allow your pain to draw you closer to God. Fight the voice in your head that tells you that your sin or your pain has disqualified you from a loving relationship with your heavenly Father. That voice is a liar! Our enemy, Satan, would love to use your sin and pain too, but he'd love to use it against you. He would love nothing more that to see you run farther from God and wallow in your pain. In the painful moments of your life, Satan will tell you that you are broken and worthless, that you will never be used by God, and that you will never be loved by God. He will tell you to run away from God.

In those moments when the guilt and shame and fear are overwhelming, remember what Jesus said about Satan, "He was a murderer from the beginning, not holding to the truth, for there is no truth in him. When he lies, he speaks his native language, for he is a liar and the father of lies" (John 8:44). When the voice inside your head tells you that your pain disqualifies you for a life with God, remind yourself, and Satan, that he is a liar. Don't believe liars.

Instead, draw near to God. Go to him in your pain and ask him for his power to overcome your pain. Ask him for comfort, ask him for forgiveness if your actions have caused the pain. Ask him for peace! One of my favorite verses in the Bible says that if we go to God with our pain, with our worries, if we ask him for help, then "the peace of God, which transcends all understanding, will guard your hearts and your minds in Christ Jesus" (Phil. 4:7).

The peace of God that transcends all understanding. Wow! That means that God's peace is so great we can't understand it! Have you ever experienced that? Have you ever felt at peace when everything in the world around you was telling you that you should be freaking out? I have. That night Chloe was in the intensive care unit, I got in the bed with her to pray with and for her. I had to leave to be with my other kids, and my wife was going to stay the night with her. I really did not want to leave, but I had to.

So I snuggled up next to her as well as I could with all of the wires and machines and sang to her and prayed for her. And in that moment, when I was so worried about my baby, I felt, in my heart, not out loud, God say to me, "Johnny, I've got her." When I got home I wrote in my journal that I knew that Chloe would be okay. I still didn't sleep well, but I had a peace that was way beyond what I understood. When you go through pain, ask God for peace. It might not come immediately, but it will come.

Then, as I mentioned, the second way to allow God to use our pain for our good is when we let him use our pain to help others. How does serving others work together for our good? We'll take a closer look at that in chapter 9. For now, just know that serving others from your pain will give your pain a purpose. Pastor Rick Warren says that our greatest ministry comes from our greatest hurts. Don't believe me? Go back and read the introduction again. Notice that my mom and dad started Celebrate Recovery because of their pain. And look at what God has done! God can do the same for, and through, you!

When you understand that God wants to use your pain to help others, you will see a purpose for your pain you never thought possible. Oh, I'm not saying that you'll ever be happy you went through pain, but you will find that when pain has a purpose, when you are being used by God to help others, you will start to look at pain differently. You'll start saying, "Okay, God, who are you going to comfort now that I've gone through this?" And don't worry, God will show you!

Pain is inevitable, but we can allow the pain we go through to have a purpose. We can allow God to use our pain to get our attention and draw us near to him. We can allow God to use our brokenness to help others around us. We can remember that God uses only broken people who have experienced pain. In the next chapter we will see that not only can God use our pain, but Jesus also cares deeply about the pain we go through. We are not alone.

Jesus cares deeply about your pain

Jesus loves me, this I know, for the Bible tells me so. Little ones to him belong; they are weak, but he is strong."

I sang that song every week in Sunday school at the church I grew up in. Every Sunday we sang about Jesus' love for us, and then we learned how to earn God's love. At least, that's how I remember it. I remember a feeling of guilt and being taught that in order for God to love me, I had to be a "good boy." I stayed at this church until my freshman year of high school. While I have many positive memories about this church because it's where I began my relationship with Jesus, I eventually left and walked away from church because I constantly worried that I couldn't live up to God's high standards.

I somehow missed the sermons about God's grace. I already had a pretty heavy conscience and felt guilty about pretty much everything. I felt guilty for feeling good, and I felt guilty for feeling bad. It was an uncomfortable place to be. I always understood justice, I always understood the God of the Old Testament. Do something wrong? Punishment. Do something right? Reward. The problem with this was that I did way more wrong than I did right. I knew I would be punished.

I still struggle against this mindset. I sometimes act as though at the end of the day, I will present a scorecard to God. Column 1 will say, "Fail" and Column 2 will say, "Win!" As long as there are more checks in Column 2, more things I did right than wrong, I'll get a gold star and a pat on the back from God. If Column 1 has more checks, watch out. Here comes a smiting!

I now understand how foolish that mindset is. Because of the grace of Jesus Christ, I don't have to worry about earning God's love. Not only do I not have to worry about it, I can never earn it. No matter how good I am, I can't earn God's love. The converse is true as well. No matter how bad I am, I can never make God stop loving me.

Bedtime Routine

Every night my kids and I go through our bedtime ritual. I climb into bed next to them, one after another, and spend a little one-on-one time with them. Right before they go to sleep, after we've sung and prayed and talked about their days, I ask them four questions. It goes like this:

"How big do I love you?"

"Huge!"

"And how long will I love you?"

"Forever."

"And what could make me stop?"

"Nothing!"

"Why not?"

"Because you're my daddy and nothing could make you stop."

I've done this with them every night for as long as I can remember. When they were younger the responses were a little more enthusiastic, but we still do it every night. I was worried my oldest might be a little too cool for it, so one night I thought I'd skip it in case she didn't have the heart to tell me she didn't want to keep doing it. I kissed her goodnight and started to leave the room. She said, "Hey! You didn't ask me the questions!" I haven't skipped it since.

I started this because I never wanted my kids to wonder if their daddy loved them. When they are being disciplined or when they are far away and they start to wonder if I love them, I want the questions to come to mind. I never wanted them to doubt that I love them. I also wanted them to draw a connection between my imperfect love for them and God's perfect love for them. God could have chosen any way to describe his relationship to us. Creator. King. Lord. Ruler. All of these fit, but it isn't the way we are told to approach him. Jesus tells us to call God, "Our Father" (Matt. 6:9).

God's preferred title for himself in relation to us is Father. When we enter into a relationship with Jesus, we are made his children. The Bible tells us, "See what great love the Father has lavished on us, that we should be called children of God! And that is what we are!" (1 John 3:1). God makes us his children, and he is our Father! When I started asking my kids our nightly questions, I wanted them to know that if their broken, imperfect, earthly father would always love them, no matter what, then their perfect, heavenly Father would love them even more! I didn't want them to miss God's grace like I did as a teen.

The Bible has often been called "God's love letter" to his children, and that is an apt description. Too often we can approach this love letter as a textbook, or, even worse, as a rule book. We can turn to Scripture as a way to see what we should or shouldn't do. There are clearly things God says we shouldn't do. That's called sin. God wants us to put him first and follow after him with our whole hearts.

For our own good he's shown us what things to avoid, things that are bad for us, things that will hurt us. He's not trying to keep us from a good time; he's giving us a way for a better life. Like a Good Father, he has placed boundaries in our lives. He's told us what to do, and what we should not do. But when we read the Bible and miss why he's given us these boundaries, we miss out on a huge picture of who God is.

Veruca Salt

God has given us this way to live because he loves us. Like I said earlier, I have three kids, Maggie, Chloe, and Jimmy. I love them in a way I can not hope to describe. I want to give them the world! But I know that because I love them, I have to place boundaries on them. I don't want them to turn out like Veruca Salt from *Willy Wonka and the Chocolate Factory*.

If you recall, Willy has invited five children to his factory to (spoiler alert) find a successor to take over for him when he retires. One of the children is Veruca Salt, a spoiled girl. Over and over, she demands that her father get her all of the wonderful things she sees in the factory. Finally, she sees geese that lay golden eggs, and she wants one of them, now.

When Mr. Wonka explains to her father, who has his checkbook in hand, that the geese are not for sale, she throws a musical tantrum: "I don't care how, I want it now!" she sings. Finally, she sits on one of the egg scales, is measured a "bad egg," and down the garbage shoot she goes. It isn't really poor Veruca's fault. She's never had boundaries. She's never been told no. She's been allowed to do what she wants, when she wants.

I don't want my kids to turn into Veruca Salt. I want them to know that there are things that are not for them, either, because they aren't good for them, or they simply aren't ready for it. For example, I am a hundred percent sure that my son would love to drive my car. The other day while riding his bike he yelled, "I'm free! Free to be a hoodlum!" Jimmy wants to go faster. He wants to play. He wants to explore. But as a nine-year-old, he is not ready to drive, and driving would not be good for him. It will be someday, but it isn't today. He needs to wait.

Since Chloe's spill on the scooter, she's not even allowed to look at her scooter without her helmet on. Am I a bad father because I've given her the rule of always wearing a helmet when she rides the scooter? No. I want her to be safe. I haven't banned scooters in our house (I was tempted to) or packaged her up in bubble wrap (again, I was tempted to), but I have given her safe boundaries. That's what God has done for us. He doesn't remove us from temptation or situations where we have to choose to follow him. He doesn't turn us into robots, but he gives us guidelines, boundaries, and rules. Some might even call them *commandments*. He does this because he loves us.

Slow down. Make sure you catch this, because if you

miss it, you'll miss out on so much about God. Take it from me; I missed this for so long. I missed it until I began recovery. Don't miss the truth that God loves you. This is so important, so fundamental that it has become cliché. Stop for a moment and allow the truth of this to become real to you. God loves you. The Creator of the universe who laid the earth's foundation and who marked its dimensions (Job 38:4–5) loves you. The One who spoke the world into existence (Genesis 1) cares about you. Don't let this rush by. Don't shrug it off. Maybe you've heard this a hundred times, but let this hundred and first be the time it overwhelms you. Not my words, but the truth that God, the God of everything, loves you.

I can so easily miss this. In my day-to-day rush, I can miss the fact that the most powerful being in the universe, the one who created that very universe, loves me. Oh, there's a part of me that "knows" he loves me, but I don't always understand it. But the rest of what follows in this book depends on this understanding. We cannot hope to recover from our hurts, hang-ups, and habits until we understand that God loves us and cares about our pain. You and I need to see God how he wants us to see him: as our loving Father. If we are going to find purpose in our pain, if we are going to overcome our issues, we need to begin to believe that God loves us. He loves us with a love we did not, and can not earn.

God's love is a product of his grace for us. The Bible clearly states that without God's intervention we would never be able to live the kind of life he intended us to live. The Bible also makes it clear that God doesn't want any of us missing out on the life he has planned for us. We were, and are, incapable of living a perfect life, but God is perfect. God can not sin. "This is the message we have heard from him and declare to you: God is light; in him there is no darkness at all" (1 John 1:5). Because God is perfect, he cannot have a relationship with those of us who are sinners. So all through history he has given his people ways to make themselves right with him. In the Old Testament God gave his people "the law," a list of rules to follow that would make them right with God.

The problem with the law is that no one can follow it. We all have a part of us that desires sin. The Bible calls this part of us our flesh, and our flesh cries out for us to do the wrong thing. So God gave his people a system where they could offer animal sacrifices to him as a way to atone for their sins. But this system required continual sacrifices, because the people continued to sin. Try as they might to do the right thing, they were imperfect people who made mistakes and sinned. Instead of making things better, the law merely pointed out how far we were from perfection (Rom. 3:20).

God changed all that with Jesus. The most famous verse in the Bible is John 3:16: "For God so loved the world that he gave his one and only Son, that whoever believes in him shall not perish but have eternal life." That verse is famous for a good reason. It states the reason Jesus stepped out of heaven and into our world. (See John 1:1 and Phil. 2:6–11.)

Jesus was with God in heaven in perfect unity. However, he decided to enter our world to save us from our sins. Jesus was born as a human being (Luke 2:1–21), was tempted to sin (Matt. 4:1–11), but never sinned and was perfect (Heb. 4:15). Jesus loved us so much he left heaven to save us. He saved us by the same system set up by God in the Old Testament: through sacrifice. This time it wouldn't be an animal sacrifice for our sins; it would be Jesus himself.

Jesus gave himself over to be crucified on a cross. After being beaten and insulted, he suffered a horrible death so that you and I could be made right with God. On the cross he took all of the sins that had been and ever would be committed and put them on himself. When Jesus was on the cross, there was a moment when God turned away from the sins that were placed on Jesus (Mark 15:34). Just before Jesus died on that cross, he declared, "It is finished" (John 19:30). Sin had been defeated. The mission Christ had come on, the mission to end our separation from God because of sin, was over. But Jesus wasn't done yet.

Three days later, after he had been buried in a sealed tomb, Jesus rose to life again (John 20)! Through his death and resurrection, Jesus defeated sin and death. Unlike the earlier system of sacrifice that needed to be made over and over, this perfect sacrifice needed to be made only once. It was a sacrifice for all people, for all of the sins we'd ever commit. It was done for us because Jesus loves us.

Deciding to Follow Jesus

If you have never made the decision to follow Christ as your personal Savior, nothing could be more important. Trusting Christ with your life is the only way to overcome your hurts, hang-ups, and habits. Following Christ is the only way to find forgiveness for your sins and life after death. If you haven't made the choice to follow Jesus, I suggest you call up someone you know who has and ask them to help you take the next step. Or you could simply say the following prayer. Don't worry about getting the words exactly right; it's more about what's going on in your heart. Just pray,

Jesus, I'm ready. I want to follow you. I have lots of questions, but I don't need all the answers to know I want you to be my Lord and Savior. I believe you are the Son of God, that you came into our world and died so I could be forgiven for my sins. You were raised back to life so that I could have life. Please come into my life, forgive me for the wrong things I've done, and help me overcome my hurts, hang-ups, and habits. Amen.

If you prayed that prayer, tell someone. Get involved at a local church if you aren't already. You'll find there aren't any perfect people there, but they will help you as you begin this journey. To find a church near you, if you don't have one already, go to www.celebraterecovery.com and click on the "How do I find a Celebrate Recovery" button. Then you can search by your area.

If you have followed Jesus for any length of time, it's still important to remember his sacrifice. From time to time I can forget how much Jesus loves me and fall into the trap of thinking I need to earn his love or I will be condemned. But John 3:17 reminds me, "For God did not send his Son into the world to condemn the world, but to save the world through him." Jesus enters our world because he loves us.

Jesus Loves You, and He Cares about Your Pain

Pain has a purpose: to get our attention and to draw us nearer to God. When we go through painful times, we need to remember Jesus loves us and cares about our pain. One of my favorite verses in the Bible is 1 Peter 5:7, "Cast all your anxiety on him because he cares for you." As someone who struggles with anxiety, this has become one of my life's verses. Instead of telling me that worry is a sin or that my faith isn't strong enough, this verse tells me to give all of my anxiety to Jesus. When I worry—and let me tell you, I can worry about anything at any time—I can give it to Jesus. Why? Because he cares about me!

When I first read this verse I had to stop and sit still for a while. Jesus cares about me. He cares about my worries; he cares about my pain. When I go to him with my struggles, he doesn't roll his eyes and put up with me; he loves me and wants to help me. He will provide a way for me to overcome my pain.

What Should We Do When We Are in Pain?

First, tell Jesus about it.

Pain can either push us away from God or it can draw us nearer to him. Jesus stepped out of heaven in a rescue mission to draw us back to him. Crying out to Jesus is the first step in drawing near to him.

You aren't going to a judge who is waiting to condemn you. You aren't going in for a scolding; you aren't going to be told, "I told you so." You're going to your *Father*. It's important to remember this when you have caused the pain you're going through. When I blow it, I tend to approach God differently. I come to him not as my Father but as a judge. I feel like I need to plead my case as to why God should forgive my sins, but then I remember: he has given me Jesus.

In Jesus I have forgiveness of sins and a restored relationship with my Father. Look at Romans 8:15: "The Spirit you received does not make you slaves, so that you live in fear again; rather, the Spirit you received brought about your adoption to sonship. And by him we cry, 'Abba, Father.'" We can turn to our Father when we are in pain. And we'll find a loving Father, our Abba, who wants us to come to him.

I'll never forget the first time my kids called me, "Dada." My wife and I disagree on whether they said Dada or Mama first, but I'll tell you the truth: it was Dada. By calling me Dada, they were showing that they understand our relationship.

I'm Dada. I'm a husband, a son, an employee, a boss, a pastor, a friend, and many other roles, but I am a daddy to just three people. My kids have a special relationship with me. When they are afraid in the night, they call for me. When they make a mistake, they come to me and talk about it. I discipline them because I love them. But I don't push them away. I don't tell them they are bad. We talk through their mistakes and discuss how they can learn from them.

Abba

Abba is the Aramaic version of Daddy, and we are told we can go to our Father God as Daddy. There's a personal, intimate relationship there. Daddy is special. When you go to God as Father, as Abba, as Daddy, you go to someone who loves you and who wants what's best for you. You go to someone who cares about your pain. You go to someone who can help you with your pain.

When we approach our Father we find power, we find mercy, and we find grace. Look at Hebrews 4:16: "Let us then approach God's throne of grace with confidence, so that we may receive mercy and find grace to help us in our time of need." When we go to God in our pain we find grace and mercy, but we also find the help we need. I love this verse because it tells me I don't have to crawl to God, like the Prodigal Son practicing my speech, to get him to love and forgive me, but I can approach him with confidence. I have confidence in my Father that he will show me compassion and grace, and I have confidence that he will help me with my pain.

The next thing to do when you are in pain is tell someone else about it. This is a huge recovery key: to overcome pain, we must share it with another person. There are days I wish this weren't a part of it. There are times when my pain feels so personal that I want to keep it to myself. There's a cliche in recovery: "You are only as sick as your secrets." The things we keep to ourselves are the things that will keep us sick. The things we keep to ourselves own us. Whether it's something we've done or something that's been done to us, when we keep secrets, they have power over us. That power keeps us stuck.

As you read this you may be thinking about something

you've done that you hope no one ever finds out about. You may have a secret that you've protected and kept hidden for so long that it feels like it's a part of you. This secret owns you.

By trying to protect our secrets, we are admitting that they need protecting. They are special and fragile and important. I know what I'm talking about because I kept my drinking a secret for so long. I knew if others knew how much and how often I drank there would be consequences. I hid my drinking from my wife so we wouldn't fight. I hid it from my parents so they wouldn't worry. I hid it from others so they wouldn't find out what a hypocrite I was. And I hid it because if others knew, I wouldn't be able to get away with it anymore.

Telling other people about our struggles leads to healing. The secret is out. The hardest time to admit you have a problem is the first time. The first time I told my wife I was an alcoholic, I was shaking and felt like I might throw up. The first time I said it in group, I was a little nervous, but talking about my secret was much easier after that. I recently had a conversation with a friend about my addiction issues, and I didn't even think twice about discussing it. That's because my addictions don't own me anymore. I have told so many people about my issues, so often, that they are out in the open. Their power over me is gone. James 5:16 says, "Therefore confess your sins to each other and pray for each other so that you may be healed." Talking about our problems to another person and praying for each other leads us to healing.

This is as true of pain we have caused as it is for the pain done to us. The Bible says that "all have sinned and fall short of the glory of God" (Rom. 3:23).

All of us have been hurt by others. We've been lied to, taken advantage of, or overlooked by people close to us. Some of us have been hurt in other, deeper ways. If you have been deeply hurt by others, if you have been abused, molested, a victim of a crime or infidelity, know that God cares deeply about that pain. If you want freedom from that pain, you'll need to give it to God first and then talk to someone else about it. You'll find your loving Father who wants to help you in your time of need. And by telling someone else about your pain, you'll begin to loosen the chains around you.

Make sure the person, or people you talk to about your pain are safe people. Just as you won't find judgment when you come to God, you want to find people who will not judge you as well. What we all need in this situation is someone who will understand us and not try to fix us. We need someone who will listen and pray, not give us solutions. We need someone who will share with us as well. We don't need a guru or an expert, but a fellow struggler who can walk alongside us on our journey. How can you find this kind of person? I'd suggest attending a Celebrate Recovery ministry if you don't already. You'll find people there who can understand what you're going through because they are going through it themselves.

If you already attend Celebrate Recovery, not only can you continue to find people to share your pain with, but you can become that kind of person for others. Make yourself available for people and meet them where they are. This is one way you can give your pain a purpose. Use your experience to help others. Listen to them, pray for them, and share your struggles and victories with them.

Jesus loves you deeply. Sometimes I forget how much he loves me, that he came to save me and not condemn me, so it helps to have a place to go to when I need a reminder. For me, it's the book of John, starting with chapter 12. In those chapters you'll see Jesus praying for you. You'll read about him loving you and dying for you. You'll read about an empty tomb. It's pretty great. Give it a try. You'll probably need it for what's coming next.

Facing your pain and mistakes is the only way to deal with them

I'm going to be honest, this is the hard part. Lots of people say recovery is hard, and usually this is the part they are referring to. Dealing with the past is hard. It isn't a lot of fun, and if it's your first time, it can feel pointless. But it is one of the keys to recovery.

The main key for success in recovery, and life, is a relationship with Jesus Christ. There are lots of things that go into a successful recovery process. Safe relationships, investing in recovery and taking it seriously, and attending meetings are just a few of them. Another one is dealing with the pain and mistakes of the past. Facing our past mistakes and pain, head on, is the only way to get it where it belongs: behind us.

In Celebrate Recovery we begin to deal with our pasts in what is called the Inventory or Principle Four. Others might refer to it as completing a Fourth Step. The process is simple, even if it's difficult to do. Completing an inventory is simply listing all of the good and bad things you've done and that have been done to you. I'll admit, most people focus more on the bad things than the good, but ideally an inventory should be balanced. We are not all good or all bad. As we explored in the previous chapter, we have all made mistakes and we have all been hurt by other people's mistakes. But we've also done good things. So an inventory is simply writing down both the good we've done and the good that's been done to us, and the bad we've done and the bad that's been done to us.

Let's focus on the negative things for a while, because it's only when we deal with our pain and mistakes that we will find freedom. When someone comes to the inventory for the first time, they are usually filled with fear and dread, because they have heard people talk about how hard it is. Again, I'm not saying it's easy, but it isn't impossible either. But often people want to skip this part. They say things like,

- "How can digging up all the pain in my past be good for me?"

- "This just doesn't make sense!"
- "Why should I even do this?"

I've heard lots of excuses and reasons from people as to why they "don't need" to do an inventory, so they are going to push fast forward and move on past it. But each person who has tried this has ended up telling me, "I don't know why, but recovery just didn't work for me." That's like saying, "I decided not to do the exercise plan that's worked so well for so many people over the years and instead I went to the gym and just hung out. Working out didn't work for me." Ridiculous!

Hundreds of thousands of men and women have gone through Celebrate Recovery, and each one who has found freedom and victory has completed not just one inventory but often more than one. These brave men and women knew that facing the past was the only way to overcome it. I've heard so many people say recovery didn't work for them and then found out that they have left out critical components that are essential for change. Let me address a few common questions about the process.

Common Questions

"How can this possibly help?" Good question. Most of this chapter will be dedicated to answering it. For now think

back to the last chapter about Jesus caring about your pain. In that chapter we talked about being "as sick as your secrets." One key reason an inventory helps is that it brings the secrets of the past into the light of the truth in the present. As we go on, we'll cover more ways that dealing with the pain in our past helps, but let's start off with this one.

"Why should I even do this?" Hundreds of thousands, if not millions, of people have done this before you. The ones who have completed an inventory have found freedom and victory, while those that skip it often fail. So let me ask you, how serious are you about your personal recovery? Put another way, how badly do you want to change? Have you tried on your own to change? Maybe you've tried willpower or gutting it out or just deciding you are different now. Has that worked? For most of us sheer willpower won't work, at least not for long.

So maybe it's time to try something different, to try writing an inventory. Why? Because it works. Because dealing with our pain and our past is the only way to freedom. In John 5, we meet an invalid who has been unable to walk for thirty-eight years. Every day he went to a special pool that was said to heal people. The water would be stirred and the first person to get in the pool would be healed. This man went there every day and waited for his chance to be first. Then Jesus showed up.

Jesus saw the man and learned how long he had been

in that condition and asked him this simple question: "Do you want to get well?"

Imagine the man's face. *Did this guy just ask me what I think he did? Do I want to get well? Why else would I come here day after day if I don't want to get well?* I bet he was a little insulted, because he defended himself, saying why he hadn't gotten well. He told Jesus that since he was unable to walk, someone always beat him into the water. Jesus responded, "Get up! Pick up your mat and walk." And the man did something incredible: he picked up his mat and walked.

The man wanted to be healed. He wanted to be healthy. He could have looked at Jesus and said, "Sure, can you put me in the water?" Or he could have made excuses about how he couldn't just pick up his mat. Instead, he got up. Now, I don't know this for sure, but it looks like this man had never met Jesus before. Scripture doesn't tell us whether Jesus' reputation had preceded him, giving this man reason to believe Jesus could actually heal him. Instead, I think this man wanted to be healed so badly that he was willing to look like a fool if Jesus couldn't actually do it. He had been trying a way to be healed, but when another way was offered, he took it.

You and I need to follow this man's example. If you have been trying to overcome a hurt, hang-up, or habit on your own power, it is time to try something new! Jesus is asking you, right now, "Do you want to get well?" If your answer is yes, it is time to deal head-on with the pain of your past.

A few years ago—once our kids were a little older and she was able to get out more—my wife completed her first Step Study in Celebrate Recovery. A Step Study is where participants go through four workbooks that walk them through the steps and principles. When the Step Study was over, Jeni told me that her favorite part had been the fourth step, the inventory. We were sitting on our couch in the living room and I burst out laughing. I had never heard anyone say this before. I noticed Jeni was not laughing. She was giving me "the look." So, being a wiser husband by now, I stopped laughing and apologized. I told her that her comment had caught me off guard. She cracked a smile and said, "I know, but hear me out." She went on to say that until she completed her inventory she didn't realize that she had never grieved her parents' divorce. She was six when they divorced, and until this time she had never allowed herself to grieve that pain. Now she was able to deal with the pain.

This conversation fundamentally changed the way I think about the inventory. For years I bought into the idea that the inventory was hard and something to be endured. Now I was starting to think there might be more to it. What if it could be enjoyed? What if I went into the inventory process not dreading it or gritting my teeth to get through it, but looking forward to what God was going to reveal to me in the process? Talk about a change of perspective!

Okay, but what if you're not in recovery? Pastor Rick Warren says there are two kinds of people in the world, those who know they need recovery and those in denial. I happen to agree with him. I'll say it this way: we all need recovery. No matter where you've been or what you've done, you need recovery. Don't worry, you won't be judged or made to do a secret handshake, just find a Celebrate Recovery in your area and show up. You'll find lots of people who have gone through this process who would love to help you.

But here's a secret: you don't have to wait until you get into recovery to learn from and apply this lesson. While completing a Celebrate Recovery inventory is the best way to deal with the pain of our pasts, it isn't where any of us begin. We begin by admitting we have pain. That's the beginning of recovery itself, and it might seem like a no-brainer, but trust me, it isn't.

This is actually the first and hardest step. Admitting you have gone through, and caused, pain is as important as admitting you have a problem, or that your life is unmanageable. In Celebrate Recovery we talk about finding freedom from our hurts, hang-ups, and habits, and those hurts, hang-ups, and habits are not limited to one area of our lives. If you are in Celebrate Recovery you most likely came for the first time when life was out of control.

As Pastor John says, we begin recovery only when the pain in our lives has become bigger than the fears we have. We may fear change, failure, or having our secrets exposed, but once the pain in our lives grows larger than those fears, we will finally seek out change and recovery.

Peeling the Onion

Most of us seek out recovery for a single area in our lives that is out of control. In my life this area was alcoholism. I knew I had to stop drinking, that it was out of control, but I had no idea how to do it. But as the recovery process goes on, many of us have learned that although we may have sought out recovery for a certain issue, we have more than one out-of-control issue in our lives. Sometimes many more. People come to Celebrate Recovery because a relationship is out of control and learn they also have food issues. People come because of drug addiction and soon learn they are also codependents. Finding true freedom from our hurts, hang-ups, and habits means that we shine the light of truth we find in Celebrate Recovery on *all* areas of our lives. So while I began Celebrate Recovery for my alcohol issues, I have learned over the years that I also struggle with codependency, food, anxiety, finances, and many other areas. I am not done with recovery yet.

We already covered much of this in Life Lesson 3, so

I won't go over it more here except to say, we are works in progress. Remember Philippians 1:6, "Being confident of this, that he who began a good work in you will carry it on to completion until the day of Christ Jesus." What we find when we admit we have issues or pain in our past is that we are at the beginning of our journey. We may attend Celebrate Recovery for one issue and then learn that there is more to the story. This is often referred to as "peeling the onion." If you've ever cut an onion you know that it is made up of many thin layers. In recovery we begin the process of peeling the onion of our lives by facing the first and most pressing issue in our lives. Then, after we find some freedom or as the pressing needs of that issue begin to move to the background, we are able to move on to the next layer, or the next issue.

What I have learned is that the deeper I dig into those layers, the closer I get to the root cause of my issues. Alcohol was and is an issue for me (while I've been sober since 2003, I know the minute I think I can handle drinking again is the moment my relapse begins), but it was not my main issue. It was my most out-of-control and pressing issue; it was the one that demanded attention. My sin addiction to alcohol was causing pain in my life and in the lives of my family members, and until I faced it head-on, it was going to continue getting worse and worse, but it was also a symptom of greater pain. There is an issue at the root of my pain that causes me to act out in any number of ways. Learning about that root, and finding out what that root is, has taken me years. I have found that, for me, anxiety is my core issue. My anxiety and worry causes me to try to find ways to comfort myself, and these behaviors often get out of control.

There's a phenomenon known as "cross addiction," and unfortunately it isn't being addicted to the cross of Christ. Cross addiction is when someone in recovery finds sobriety in one issue, but instead of applying recovery to all areas of their lives soon finds a new addiction in a new area. Cross addiction happens when we apply the truth of recovery to the symptoms instead of the roots. This is like adding layers to the onion instead of peeling them back. People find freedom from sexual addiction but begin drinking to cover the pain. Instead of acting out with alcohol, ice cream becomes the way to cover pain. As relationships get healthy, spending becomes out of control. All of these ways of trying to cover pain, or what some call self-medicating, happen because the root issue is never dealt with.

For example, when we moved in, our house had a tiny sloped back yard covered with vines. At first we thought the vines were pretty, so we left them alone. Then we discovered that rats lived under the vines, so we decided to pull up the vines to get rid of the rats. Now we had a dirt-covered slope—at least for a while, until the weeds grew in. And soon we had a problem.

One Saturday my wife and I went outside to pull the weeds, and we were soon discouraged. There were just so many of them! So we decided to make it fun. We'd see who could clear the most weeds in an hour. When we called it quits for the day, we felt pretty good about what we'd accomplished.

Later that week it rained. The next weekend we came out to tackle another part of the slope and were shocked to find that the weeds we had pulled last weekend were not only back, but they were bigger than ever. Why? Because in our hurry to pull as many weeds as possible, we stopped actually pulling them and started trimming them. By all appearances, the weeds were gone, but the roots remained under the soil. Given the right stimulus, in this case rain, they grew right back, bigger and badder than ever.

Our issues are a lot like these weeds. Until we begin working on the root issues, our hurts, hang-ups, and habits will come back, either in the same old ways or in different new ones. To find healing, real healing, we need to have the courage to peel back the onion and deal with what we find. Again, this is a process. The process begins when we take the first step and admit we have a problem, then we move forward and dig deeper and deeper until we find the root of our pain. All along the way we deal with our pain head-on. When we do, we find the road to freedom.

Are you feeling run-down? Are you running on empty?

Do you feel like no matter how hard you try, the weeds just keep growing back? It might be that you have not dealt with something —a pain in the past, a mistake you made years ago, or an out-of-control behavior. This realization can happen to any of us at any time. You may be checking out recovery or have been in recovery for years when you discover some issues in your life you haven't faced.

I want this to be very clear. The mistakes we've made in the past, and the things others have done to us that caused us pain in the past, belong in the past. You have undoubtedly heard the phrase "One day at a time." One day at a time means that we don't live too far off in the future, worrying about what is to come. But it also means that we don't live stuck in the past. We have to deal with the past so we can become free of it.

So how do we do this? First, we admit there is an issue. Many of us stop right here. Coming out of denial can be uncomfortable, because we are popping the bubble of fantasy that shields us. We pretend our lives are perfect and nothing is out of control. We pretend the pain we went through as children wasn't that big of a deal. We compare our behavior to others and pride ourselves that at least we aren't as bad as they are. We fear exposing the family secret or showing people our true selves, so we stay stuck. We accept a life of fantasy where we do everything we can to avoid the truth so we can be "happy." But we aren't happy. We are afraid.

I have a friend who won't go to the doctor for checkups or even physicals. Why? Because people find out they are sick when they go to the doctor. If he doesn't go, he can't find out he's sick. I have another friend who won't watch the news because she doesn't want to see all of the bad things going on in the world. I have to say, I don't fault her too much for this. I think they should call the nightly news "The Evening Bad News," since that's pretty much all they show. But the bad things in the world don't stop happening just because she doesn't watch the news. Maybe you don't do these things, but many of us have left a voicemail unlistened to or an email unread because we weren't sure we wanted to know what they contained.

Not too long ago I was in complete denial about our finances. We weren't in debt, but we weren't honoring God completely with our money either. Every once in a while I'd go to the grocery store and swipe my debit card and hold my breath, just hoping there'd be enough money to cover the groceries. I wouldn't check my bank account balance because I was afraid of bad news. This was stupid. I lived this way because I didn't have the guts to do a little thing called a budget. Again, this was stupid.

Finally, I decided to get my financial house in order. So my wife and I sat down and began working through a program to address our finances. We made some simple changes, like a monthly budget and some cuts to eating out and other expenses, and all of a sudden I wasn't afraid anymore. I didn't get a raise or more income, but I knew the truth, and I was no longer living in fear that things were worse than they really were. We were able to increase our tithe, and as we began honoring God with our finances, we saw more blessings come in. Don't get me wrong, we didn't get wealthy. Our blessings weren't financial, but they were relational: Jeni and I grew closer through the process. The truth was better than the fear. And it was even better than the fantasy that everything was okay and nothing needed to change.

Taking Inventory

To find freedom from the pain of your past, you must see your past as it really is, not as you wish it was. As I said earlier, the best way I know to do this is by taking an inventory of your life. Taking an inventory is really just listing all of the things that have happened to you, remembering both the good and the bad, so you can see what is really going on in your life.

Before I was called into ministry, I worked for a restaurant, and I loved it. In the course of five years, I worked my way from a busboy all the way to manager, and I was sure I had found my calling. I really enjoyed most aspects of the job, but there was one thing in particular I did not like, and that was our daily line check.

You'd think working in a restaurant would be great because you could eat good food every day, and yes, that's a nice perk, but the line check was pretty miserable. Here's what we'd do: every shift the manager on duty would grab a bunch of spoons and head into the kitchen, or "the line." We'd take the spoons and dip them into the individual ingredients that went into the dishes the cooks would prepare. So on a typical line check you'd eat marinara sauce, plain lettuce, chicken, ranch dressing, jalapeños, partially cooked pasta, tortilla chips, pepperoni, raw onions, sautéed onions, garlic, sausage, garbanzo beans, and much more.

In the right dish some of those things work together brilliantly. On spoons, sometimes at 6:00 a.m., it tastes awful. But it is essential. The only way to know the ranch dressing hasn't spoiled is to taste it. The only way to make sure no one would get sick, or that old ingredients weren't being used, was to go through them one by one. This "daily inventory" helped us see the food for what it really was, not for what we hoped or assumed it was.

This is true in life as well. Taking the time to do an inventory, taking the time to see your life for what it really is, is essential in helping you move forward into what God has planned for you. The absolute best way to do this is to join a Celebrate Recovery Step Study, but if you can't or won't do that, you can begin this process by asking yourself some tough questions. This whole process begins with the willingness to explore, to seek answers. As you read through these questions you might feel like they are too hard, or that you don't have the power to do this. That's okay. The power we need doesn't come from ourselves at all. The power we need comes from Jesus. Remember, "Jesus looked at them and said, 'With man this is impossible, but with God all things are possible'" (Matt. 19:26).

If you have not yet attended Celebrate Recovery, ask yourself these questions:

- What one thing do I hope no one ever finds out about?
- What was I never allowed to talk about as a child?
- Are there any events of my childhood that haunt me today?
- Do I have any out-of-control behaviors or tendencies?
- How am I trying to cover my pain?
- What events of my past shaped me?
- Why am I resisting getting the help I need?

I would suggest writing your answers out on paper, because something about seeing them in black and white helps make the answers real. As you answer these questions, if you find you'd like some help dealing with your pain, please visit: www.celebraterecovery.com to find a Celebrate Recovery ministry in your area. You don't have to face your pain alone!

If you are already in Celebrate Recovery, ask yourself these questions:

- Are there layers of the onion I have not dealt with?
- What issue brought me to Celebrate Recovery? How am I doing in that area?
- Have I begun the process of digging out the weeds by the root, or am I just trimming them?
- What steps do I need to take to deal with the other hurts, hang-ups, and habits in my life?

Whether it is an unpaid bill, a medical diagnosis, or any other painful situation in our lives, dealing with it head-on is the only way to get through it. Leaving the bill on the table doesn't get it paid; it adds late fees. Avoiding medical treatment doesn't cure disease; it allows it to fester and get worse. And avoiding facing the pain of our past doesn't make it go away. Just like cancer, if our pain is left untreated, it will grow and get worse and worse. The first step is to see our pain clearly, to write it down and face it. Then we can take action on it.

One word of caution: don't go through this alone. Get around other people and ask for help. Attend Celebrate

Recovery, get a counselor, or lean on trusted friends to help you through this process. The Bible says, "Two are better than one, because they have a good return for their labor: If either of them falls down, one can help the other up. But pity anyone who falls and has no one to help them up. Though one may be overpowered, two can defend them-selves. A cord of three strands is not quickly broken" (Eccl. 4:9–10, 12). Get some people around you for help. By facing your pain, and by taking action on it, you will find freedom you may have never thought was possible.

Keeping short accounts is necessary for relational change

We have all gone through pain in our lives. Some of the pain was our fault, our sinful actions causing pain in our lives and in the lives of others, and some of the pain was the result of the actions of other people. The process of finding freedom from the pain of our past begins when we start to see our past as it really is. By writing it down and taking an inventory of all of the good and the bad, we start to see the truth in our lives. Fantasy and fear is replaced by truth. Jesus said, "Then you will know the truth, and the truth will set you free" (John 8:32). To be set free from the pain in your past, you must see the past as it really is.

But there's another component to finding freedom: taking action. Knowing the truth, but not acting on it, will not set you free; it will make you miserable! Much of our pain comes from relationships. I wish this wasn't true, but so much of the pain we encounter comes from people around us. Because we are involved with people, spouses, children, parents, coworkers, and friends, we have hurt and will hurt other people. And we have been and will be hurt by others. To do our part in making our relationships healthy, we need to keep short accounts by making amends and offering forgiveness.

Short Accounts

The first time I heard about keeping short accounts in relationships, I was at a student leadership conference. One of the speakers told us that we needed to make apologies and forgive people quickly so we didn't carry pain around and become resentful. Being the sophisticated teenagers that we were, we took this advice to the extreme, punching each other in the arm, then bowing to each other and apologizing immediately. As teenagers we didn't really get it, but the concept has stayed with me. Short accounts are essential to maintaining good relationships.

Short accounts are built into Celebrate Recovery. We are told to take "a daily inventory and when we (are) wrong, promptly admit it" (Step 10 of the Christ-centered Twelve Steps). I'm not a huge fan of two of the words in this step. I wish instead of *when* it said *if*, and instead of *promptly* it said *eventually*. This step tells me two things: first, I *will* be wrong; it isn't a question of maybe. I'm going to do the wrong thing. Probably often. The second thing it tells me is that as soon as I realize I'm wrong, I need to admit it. That's keeping short accounts. When we promptly make amends and offer forgiveness, we don't allow problems to fester.

Think of a game of telephone. One person starts off with a simple phrase, and they whisper that phrase to the person next to them. Then that person whispers what they heard to the next person until the phrase has traveled around the group. The last person says the phrase out loud to see how well the original phrase held up. Spoiler alert: it usually doesn't hold up well. Holding on to past pain and letting it grow is kind of like that game. We allow small issues to grow into things that can choke and kill our relationships. Sometimes we will be hurt in big ways—someone will leave us, or neglect or abuse us—but other times small issues can spin out of control and become bigger than they need to be.

I have become notorious in my family for sending a text that says, "You okay?" if I'm having a hard time deciphering what someone is trying to communicate to me. It usually goes like this:

I write, "Hey, want to get lunch?"

They reply, "Sure."

"Cool, where?"

"I don't care."

"You okay?"

"Yes, Johnny. Why do you always do this?"

"Just checking."

If we were having a conversation in person, I'd know what they meant by "I don't care" because I could see it in their facial expression or hear it in their tone of voice, but over text I read all sorts of things into their reply. They probably mean they don't care where we eat, but they could mean they don't care about me. Or maybe they sighed when they typed that because of course Johnny cares where we eat, or maybe they don't think I will care where they want to eat because I'm just going to pick a place anyway. It's exhausting living in my head. It's gotten to the point that my wife ends pretty much every text with a smiley face so I know she's smiling when she replies to my messages.

We do things like this all the time.

- "Did she not say hello because she hates me, or did she not hear me?"
- "Did that guy just give me a dirty look? What did I do to him?"
- "Of course she overreacted. That's just like her."

- "Oh, him, he's just a jerk. He's always been like that."
- "I don't talk to my dad about my life because he didn't care when I was a kid."

These thoughts start off small, but eventually they can destroy a relationship. Relationships take work. Of course marriage takes work, and that is a very important relationship, but relationships with parents take work, and relationships with kids take work too. We have to work on friendships, relationships with our neighbors and coworkers, and pretty much everyone we come into contact with on a semiregular basis.

People are often amazed that my dad and I can work so well together. I think a lot of fathers and sons would have a hard time spending so much time together. People tell me, "I could never work so closely with my dad." I've never heard someone tell me that about their son. After hearing this so often and after spending so many hours in recovery group circles with men, I've come to understand that the father-son relationship is fraught with issues. Fatherhood is also extremely easy to screw up.

Please know, I'm not saying that motherhood is not important, nor am I saying that the mother-child relationship is not important. It is. My mom and my wife are two of the most amazing people I know, and I wouldn't be the person I am today without each of them. But over and over again, I hear men say that they either didn't or still don't have a good relationship with their father. Many people around my age grew up with absent fathers. While my dad was around for my childhood physically, he was emotionally unavailable for much of my early years. He coached my baseball teams and came to important events. He never hit me or abused me in any way. But there were seasons when he wasn't there.

When my parents separated, there were periods when I didn't see my dad often. As he got healthier, he started showing up more, and I was so excited to get his attention. I'll never forget when he made his amends to me. He sat me down and told me he was an alcoholic. He said he was sorry for his actions. Two thoughts went through my mind. First, the idea of his being an alcoholic didn't jibe with what I thought an alcoholic looked like. My dad was a white-collar guy. He had good jobs. In my mind, an alcoholic looked more like a hobo. The other thought was astonishment that he wasn't making excuses or blaming anyone. He wasn't making the usual promises, like, "This time, I mean it!" He was just saying sorry. I forgave him immediately.

Since then, he and I have grown closer. When I came to him with my own drinking issues, he was forgiving and loving and tender to me. He pointed me in the right direction, but he didn't chastise me or tell me what to do. He let me figure it out. I can't imagine how hard this must have been for my dad. To watch me go down the same road he had traveled, and to watch me repeat the same mistakes he had made must have been devastating. Now things are amazing. I get to work with and follow my hero. We have fun together. We don't always see eye to eye, but our relationship is genuinely strong and healthy. We have a good relationship because he modeled making amends. He modeled offering forgiveness. He, like he has done so often, showed me the way.

If you want to change a broken relationship, you must keep short accounts and acknowledge when you've blown it.

When You've Blown It

Sin has consequences. When I was active in my addiction to alcohol, I hurt people in many ways. I lied to my wife and others around me. I hid my drinking and isolated myself from those close to me. I put people in compromising situations when I asked people to lie on my behalf. I drove under the influence of alcohol and endangered others on the road. When I started recovery, I felt ashamed. How could I have done these things? How could I have hurt my wife like that? How could I have driven in that condition? Some of my past pain was my fault.

Maybe you find yourself in a similar situation. You look

around and see a wake of destruction behind you. Maybe you feel ashamed of the things you have done, and you feel like God and others will never be able to forgive you. You're wrong. If the pain in your past was caused by your actions, you must face it head-on by asking for forgiveness. In recovery we call this making amends. Making amends is simply apologizing for the wrong we have done. It's often harder than it sounds, but by coming clean and admitting our mistakes, we begin the process of leaving those mistakes in the past.

My kids, like most kids, are bad at making apologies. They are amazing kids, but like lots of brothers and sisters, they fight. A lot. We have tried to teach our kids to apologize when they hurt each other, and they do, but usually not in the way we would hope. They groan, or say, "I'm sorry" in a tone that isn't very apologetic.

I'm not so good at apologies either. I often want to explain myself or excuse my actions. It isn't easy to simply offer an apology and leave it there. Usually I want to give some excuses or reasons. Have you ever noticed that when *you* need to apologize, you have *reasons* for your actions, but when *others* need to apologize to you they are full of *excuses*? Funny how that works, isn't it? Maybe the worst apology we can offer is one we hear a lot from celebrities and politicians when they say something offensive. You've heard it before. "I'm sorry you got offended," or "I'm sorry you took it that way." I hate that kind of apology!

When we face our mistakes and make amends for the harm we have done to others, the best way to do it is simply and without excuses. If the person wants to talk it out, I may offer my reasons or explain my thought process, but I've learned that most of the time it's better to just offer the amends.

As you deal with the pain of your past and realize you have done some things that have caused yourself and others pain, you can either feel ashamed about your mistakes or you can make amends for them. Your enemy, the devil, would like nothing more than for you to wallow in your mistakes and to feel ashamed for the rest of your life. He would like for you to replay the sins of your past over and over in your mind until you feel so stuck that you won't be available to be used by God to help others.

Jesus said, "The thief comes only to steal and kill and destroy; I have come that they may have life, and have it to the full" (John 10:10). Satan can steal, kill, and destroy you by reminding you of all the times you've blown it. But Jesus came to give you life. Choose to follow Jesus and offer amends when you've hurt other people. In doing so, you will find freedom from your past mistakes.

Not everyone will accept your amends or forgive you. I wish I could give you the formula for what to say and how to say it so that everything would be okay, but I don't have it. Some people accepted my amends, and others have told me no thank you. You cannot make anyone forgive you. That's not up to you. That is up to them.

In recovery we often talk about cleaning up "my side of the street." I can do my work, but I can't make you do yours. You may have family members who refuse your apology and instead choose to remind you of all of your past mistakes. Keeping short accounts isn't about what response you get. It's about making the effort to reach out and make amends. I hope the people you've hurt are willing to forgive you, but they might not be. Take the necessary action for your part in making the relationship right.

Apologies work best when they are accompanied with change. Like we saw in the chapter about slow, progressive growth, the changes in our lives will demonstrate that we are different. Making amends does this too. When you sit down with someone and make amends, without offering excuses, you are illustrating your change. When you learn from your mistakes and change, you are giving solid evidence that you are different.

If you have taken the step of making amends for the harm you've caused in the past, but you, the enemy, or others continue to remind you of all the ways you've blown it, these verses can be helpful to remember:

- "As far as the east is from the west, so far has he removed our transgressions from us" (Ps. 103:12).

- "If we confess our sins, he is faithful and just and will forgive us our sins and purify us from all unrighteousness" (1 John 1:9).
- "When you were dead in your sins and in the uncircumcision of your flesh, God made you alive with Christ. He forgave us all our sins, having canceled the charge of our legal indebtedness, which stood against us and condemned us; he has taken it away, nailing it to the cross" (Col. 2:13–14).

Christ died to free you from your sins. When you turn to him in repentance and make amends to others, you can find freedom from your past mistakes. Christ has already been crucified and your sins were nailed to that cross. If you have accepted his sacrifice it's time to leave those mistakes where they belong, in the past.

When Others Have Hurt You

We have all hurt others, and we have all been hurt by others. Most of us carry around hurts that were done to us by people we trusted and loved, people who never should have hurt us. All of us can think of a time we were lied to, gossiped about, judged, or left out. We cannot escape getting hurt by others. Sometimes people hurt us accidentally, and sometimes they do it on purpose. Most of us can get past the accidental hurt, but when someone hurts us on purpose, it can be much harder to understand.

If you have been abused, mistreated, molested, or in some other way hurt or victimized, I want you to know it breaks my heart that you went through that kind of trauma. It breaks God's heart too. Please know that it was not his plan for you to be hurt in that way. God can use and redeem that pain, but he hates that it happened! Psalm 56:8 tells us that God keeps a record of our tears. He knows the pain you have gone through. He can help you overcome that pain, leave it in the past, and move forward. He can put you on the road to freedom.

No matter the degree of the pain caused to you, though, you must forgive those who hurt you. I'll let that sink in for a minute. For you and me to be free from the pain done to us by others, we need to forgive them. That doesn't always seem fair to me. I didn't cause the pain, so why should I have to do anything at all? Shouldn't *they* have to pay for the pain they've caused? What if they aren't even sorry? Do I have to forgive them in that case? Well, yes. The way to freedom from the pain caused to me is forgiveness. It's the only way forward. If I refuse to forgive the people who have hurt me, I allow them to continue to have control over me. They trap me in my pain and they own me.

I bet right now you're thinking of someone who has hurt you. You can remember what they did or what they said that hurt you. If the pain was deep enough, you might have some memories of what you were wearing or where you were when it happened. That moment is frozen in your memory, and even thinking of it can cause you more pain. What if you could find freedom from that? What if you were able to move past that pain? It's possible, but it isn't easy. Forgiveness is a process that takes time and practice.

Time doesn't heal all wounds. It would be nice if it did, but it doesn't. Time can make things worse. Just last week I woke up with a sore throat and a stuffy nose. I could feel a whopper of a cold coming on. Did I go to the doctor? No, I got some vitamin C and some cough drops and decided I'd fight it off. But I wasn't getting any better. Finally I decided, after my wife told me to, to go to the doctor. He came in the room, felt my neck, looked at my chart, and said I had walking pneumonia. I was able to upgrade a cold to walking pneumonia. He put me on so many antibiotics the pharmacist thought it was a mistake. I got better, but had I not received a diagnosis and taken medication, I would have been sick a lot longer. Time did not heal my illness, and time will not heal the wounds of your past. Only forgiveness will do that.

If the pain you are dealing with happened to you as a child, a significant amount of time has passed already. You may not have had the tools to face that pain before now, but you can choose to not allow more time to pile up. If the pain is more recent, make the choice to take action now. Time will allow grudges and resentment to fester and grow. These resentments will choke the life out of you. Don't allow someone who hurt you in the past keep hurting you now.

Forgiveness is a process. Lots of people think we need to "forgive and forget" when people hurt us, but I have found that the people who want me to forgive and forget are the people who have hurt me! These people are mistaking the way God forgives us with the way we are able to forgive. I don't believe it is possible to forget some of the things done to us. I can forget the slights or the unintentional unkindnesses, but abuse or intended harm is a much harder thing to forget. What I can do is forgive. I may have to forgive the people who have hurt me more than once. I think that's okay.

I can always tell when I *think* I have forgiven someone, but I really haven't. I'll be in the middle of something mindless, doing the dishes or something, and I'll find myself arguing with that person in my head. I'll be going over the things I'd love to say to them if they ever had the guts to talk about it. I'd lay into them and tell them what I really feel. I've had this happen to me many times as I've dealt with someone who deeply hurt my wife. I would fantasize about being able to tell them off. Then I would remember I had already forgiven them. Or had I? Every time this happened, I would have to stop and pray and ask God for his power to help me forgive this person. I would ask him to remind me that this person had hurts, hang-ups, and habits just like I do. Then I would forgive them again.

This process of forgiveness repeated itself over and over again. I can say now that I have forgiven this person, but I still remember what they did. I still don't trust them the way I used to. But I don't carry that pain around anymore. I can think about them today and pray that good things happen for and to them. I can have a relationship with them.

It is very helpful to think about Jesus and what he has done for us. We know that Jesus died for our sins and that he forgives us when we repent and ask him for forgiveness. That's called grace. I don't think I can think of a single time when I have had to ask for forgiveness from a certain sin once and then changed immediately. Usually, I have had to go to Jesus multiple times in repentance and ask for forgiveness. Do you think he has a limit? Do you think there's ever been a time when he said, "Nope. That's one too many. You're done."

Thank goodness the answer is a resounding no! Jesus taught us to pray, "And forgive us our debts, as we also have forgiven our debtors" (Matt. 6:12). He didn't say, "Forgive us our debts unless we've asked thirteen times." He also instructed us to forgive people every time they ask for it. Peter asked Jesus how many times he needed to forgive someone who sinned against him. He said, "Up to seven times?" I love Peter. I can just see him puffing his chest out, acting so proud that he would allow up to seven slights. But Jesus said, "I tell you, not seven times, but seventy-seven times" (Matt. 18:22). I don't think Jesus was saying a literal seventy-seven times. I don't think he'd say, "On seventy-eight you can write them off!" I think he was taking Peter's number and blowing it out of the water. I mean, can you imagine having a little card where you mark off the number of times you've forgiven someone and when it gets to seventy-eight, you yell, "I don't think so!"?

Jesus was saying, "Keep on forgiving them." He didn't give qualifications. He didn't say, "Forgive them only if they ask" or "Forgive them for the little sins but not for the biggies." He didn't say we should forgive them if we feel like it. He just told us to forgive and keep on forgiving. He reminded us that we have been, and will continue to be, forgiven for so much. The Bible tells us, "Bear with each other and forgive one another if any of you has a grievance against someone. Forgive as the Lord forgave you" (Col. 3:13) and "Be kind and compassionate to one another, forgiving each other, just as in Christ God forgave you" (Eph. 4:32). Jesus has forgiven us, so we need to forgive others.

Jesus commands us to forgive others. He said, "For if you forgive other people when they sin against you, your heavenly Father will also forgive you. But if you do not forgive others their sins, your Father will not forgive your sins"

(Matt. 6:14–15). Jesus said we have to forgive other people. It isn't up for debate. However, he never said we had to *trust* those people again.

Trust and forgiveness are two very different things. Forgiveness can be given immediately; trust takes time to rebuild. Forgiveness is something we give to other people freely; trust must be earned. If you have been hurt by others, even if that pain is deep, you must forgive them if you are a follower of Jesus, but you don't have to trust them. You don't have to allow them to keep hurting you. You can get yourself safe and build boundaries that keep them from hurting you in the future. Forgiving the people that have hurt us is less about them and more about us. When you forgive someone for hurting you in the past, you are preventing them from continuing to hurt you in the present.

If a relationship is past the point of healing, if you have been victimized in a way that makes the person unhealthy for you, then forgiveness moves you out of the past and into the future. But if a broken relationship is going to be restored, forgiveness must be an ingredient. There can be no growth without forgiveness. If you want to do your part in restoring a relationship, then keeping short accounts and forgiving is an essential part of it. No one is saying forgiveness is easy, but it *is* necessary.

What I have seen, both in my life and in the lives of those I've counseled and walked alongside of, is that the people who excel at keeping short accounts have the greatest success in healing broken relationships. The people who can do this will find great relational change, and will influence those in their relationships to keep short accounts as well. Those who cannot offer forgiveness and make amends find that their relationships suffer. Learning to make amends and offer forgiveness quickly, thereby keeping short accounts, is crucial for relational change.

People are hurting in ways you may never see or know

About twice a month I get to travel and teach churches and leaders about how to start and grow a Celebrate Recovery ministry. We call these events "One Days," even though they take four days to pull off. We have a day of travel to get there, a setup day, the event day itself, and then another travel day. We've racked up thousands of miles of air travel and have met thousands of amazing men and women who care so deeply about the people in their communities and churches. "One Days" are a highlight of our ministry.

When I travel, there's one moment on every flight that

stands out to me: the landing. If you have ever flown into John Wayne Airport in Orange County, you know the landing approach happens over two of our busiest freeways, the 5 and the 405. These two freeways split a little south of the airport and become two congested routes. When you land at John Wayne, you cross over both of them. It doesn't matter what time your flight arrives, there will be traffic. Not only are there countless cars on the road, but you'll also fly over apartments, hotels, and homes. There are thousands upon thousands of people going about their lives. And in the span of a few seconds, from high above, you'll get a glimpse into a tiny segment of their lives.

The reason this moment stands out to me is that it is one of the very few moments I am aware of how many people are in this world. In that moment I realize I am not the center of the universe. The world opens up and I see that my life, the life of my closest circle, my friends and family, the people I interact with on a regular basis, are not the only lives that matter. Don't judge me. We all forget that we are not the most important people in the world. If life was a movie, each of us would certainly be the star!

In the Background

Back in the late nineties I moved to Hollywood to pursue an acting career. It was miserable. I'd go into auditions and see the casting director glance up, make a note, and say "next," often before I was finished with the lines. The roles I was auditioning for at the time were small, often commercials, where the director was casting a "look." If you didn't look right, they moved on until they found someone who did.

My biggest claim to fame was a few "extra" roles in some movies. I won't tell you the names of them, because even if you could find them, you'd never see me. If you don't know what an extra is, another term used for extras is "background." Are the stars talking over coffee in a diner? The extras are the people in the background. They don't have lines, they aren't referenced. They are the other customers, the waitress, the person next to the stars. If a movie didn't have extras it would be very strange. The world is full of people, so movies need to be as well. But in a movie, we are watching one or two people. We are focused on the lives of the stars. They are interesting; they have problems and conflict. They are either funny or tragic, but they are special. In the movie of our own lives, none of us would cast ourselves as extras; we are the stars! The camera is focused on us; we are the important people in the scene.

Sometimes I'll watch a movie and find an extra in the background and wonder what his story is. Is he having a bad day too? Is he enjoying that cup of coffee? Why is he in the diner anyway? Don't they all have stories? Don't they matter? If the stars got up and left, but the camera stayed, what else would we see? I do that when I watch a movie, but I rarely do that in my own life. I get impatient waiting in line because I'm in a hurry and what I have to do is important. I don't have time to wait around all day! When someone is speeding on the freeway, cutting in and out of traffic, I get huffy and say, "Someone thinks he's important," but when I do it, there's an emergency and everyone should just get out of my way.

I walk by countless strangers, sometimes nodding hello, sometimes smiling in passing, sometimes even saying, "How are you doing," but never stopping to hear the answer. I bet you do the same thing. We are all busy, we have things going on, we are the stars of our own movies.

But take a look around. If you are in a public place right now, put down the book for a minute and look at the people around you. If you're alone, the next time you go out, try this exercise. Look around and see the other people. Just look around and notice them. How do people look? My guess is that everyone is putting on a brave face. You probably won't see anyone crying or screaming out. Lots of people will just be looking at their phones. But just take a minute and notice.

What did you see? Was there a couple having a discussion? How did they look? Happy, stressed, in the middle of an argument? Did the people looking at their phones look interested or bored? Was anyone smiling or laughing? Did anyone look tired, or sad, or angry? Chances are it was all pretty boring, standard stuff. You probably didn't witness a fistfight or a breakup. You probably didn't see a marriage proposal or a baby taking their first steps. It was probably just life. But no matter what you witnessed, I can guarantee you one thing: every person you saw was in some kind of pain.

The People around You Are Hurting

The people around us are hurting. They are hurting in ways we may never see or know. They might do a fantastic job of pretending that they aren't, but they are hurting. Paul tells us in Philippians, "Do nothing out of selfish ambition or vain conceit. Rather, in humility value others above yourselves, not looking to your own interests but each of you to the interests of the others" (Phil. 2:3–4). When we do that, when we look out for the interests of others, we begin to see that they are hurting. When we acknowledge that other people have pain, a couple of interesting things can happen.

First, when I realize other people are hurting too, it makes them easy to take. Have you ever met a "sandpaper" person? I didn't come up with the term, I'm not sure who did, but it's an accurate description of some people. A sandpaper person is someone who rubs you the wrong way. They are hard to be around. If you threw a party you wouldn't invite them. Sandpaper people are either completely different from you, or they are just way too similar to you.

While sandpaper people are hard to love, God has placed them in your life for a reason. Believe it or not, sandpaper people smooth down our rough edges. I haven't spent a lot of time in a woodshop, but I have done my share of painting around the house. Sometimes, in a hurry to get a job done, I'll skip the sandpaper step. The wall, or the banister, looks smooth enough. I never complained about it being rough before, right? So on goes the paint, and it turns out horribly. There are clumps and brush marks and all manner of visible flaws. Why? Because I didn't smooth down the area first. God has placed sandpaper people in our lives to help us smooth down our rough spots.

He's also placed them in our lives to teach us to love better. All of us are good at loving people who love us. But it can be difficult to love people who are unlike us, or people we don't want to be around. Jesus said, "If you love those who love you, what reward will you get? Are not even the tax collectors doing that? And if you greet only your own people, what are you doing more than others? Do not even pagans do that?" (Matt. 5:46–47).

He also said, "A new command I give you: Love one another. As I have loved you, so you must love one another. By this everyone will know that you are my disciples, if you love one another" (John 13:34–35). Jesus wants us to love each other, but he doesn't want us to just love a subset of people. He wants us to love well. He places sandpaper people in our lives to help us love better.

Realizing people are in pain also makes it easier to forgive them when they hurt us. As we covered earlier, forgiveness is a process, and it isn't always easy. But when I see that other people are flawed and have been hurt by others, it makes them easier to forgive. Notice, I didn't say it makes it *easy* to forgive them, but it makes it *easier*. Just as you have been hurt, so have other people. No one is perfect.

My youth pastor used to repeat this saying a lot: "Hurt people, hurt people." Sometimes, you and I will be hurt by people who have been hurt by other people. Then you and I can turn around and hurt people out of our hurt. It's a cycle that keeps on going, unless we take action. When you realize people around you have been hurt, it makes them easier to forgive because you see that they are not perfect. They are just like you. Many of us have the experience of realizing our parents aren't perfect. When we come to terms with this we can actually stop holding them up to such high standards. They are just people.

When my oldest daughter was in kindergarten, she stayed home one night with my mom while my wife and I walked to school to attend our first parent-teacher informational night. On the half mile walk, Jeni and I talked about how weird it was that our baby was in kindergarten. Then I said, "When you were Maggie's age, didn't you think your parents had this all figured out? I have no idea what I'm doing!"

We laughed about this, but we also felt it very deeply. We do the best we can for our kids, but most of the time we are making it up as we go along. My parents did too. So did yours. Now, I'm not excusing neglect or abuse. I'm not saying your parents didn't know better, so their hitting you or hurting you on purpose was okay. Not at all. That is sinful behavior they will need to repent from, and you will have to forgive them in order to find healing. But for the most part, we need to recognize that people around us, including our parents, have been or are in pain. Recognizing this helps us forgive them when they hurt us.

Noticing other people's pain also keeps us from feeling isolated and alone. If you are going through a painful time it is tempting to feel like no one has gone through what you are going through right now. You may feel like everyone else in your life is happy and whole and enjoying life while you are hurting. The truth is, everyone goes through painful times. Some people's pain is deeper than others, but no one goes through life pain free. This, by the way, is one of the key strengths of Celebrate Recovery. When we get together with others and express our pain, we see that we are not alone. Other people have gone through what we are going through. Other people are experiencing the same kind of issues and pain we are.

Over the years I've had people tell me that no one has been as bad as they are, or has seen what they have seen, or has done what they have done. I've had people tell me no one has been through what they have been through. I smile and let them know I understand how they feel that way, but they aren't the first person to say this to me. I have sat in Celebrate Recovery groups in prisons with murderers, and I have sat with soccer moms who spend too much money at the mall, and I know firsthand both are in pain. Their issues look very different, the way they have coped with their pain is different, but they both feel isolated and alone.

When I notice that others are in pain, I don't feel so alone in my pain. A few years ago I went through a season of depression. For about four months I struggled to get out of bed. I stayed sober, I kept working and doing my everyday life, but I was hurting. Life had little meaning to me, and everything felt pointless. I began to ask God tough questions and felt very little in the way of answers. I'd pray and feel my prayers evaporate before I felt like they reached God. I was lost. Every day I'd get out of bed and just wonder if anything mattered. I began to fear death, or maybe just feel its inevitability, and wonder why I should try and do anything at all. Why eat healthy or work out if I was going to die anyway? Why worry about my kids or being a good parent if it wasn't going to last? I began to question everything.

I felt lost and alone. I felt weak and stupid for feeling the way I did. I had a great job and was surrounded by a loving family, so why was I depressed? I kept my feelings to myself for months, not even telling Jeni because I didn't want to worry her. Finally, after sleepless nights and meaningless days, I told my dad and then Jeni. I waited for the depression to lift, thinking that now that I talked about it, it would go away, but it didn't. But I was able to talk about it more. After revealing my depression to them, and being loved and not judged by them, I felt stronger and was able to talk to others about it. I started counseling and found help through a godly man. The more I talked about my depression, the easier it got to talk about. And the more people I told, the more people I met that struggled with similar feelings.

Thankfully, my depression lifted. I know that staying active in my personal recovery and seeking out professional help were instrumental in my healing process. God worked through others to help me in my pain. Now when I feel the fingers of depression start tightening around my neck (that's how I express it because it choked the life out of me for months), I have tools to fight against it. One of those tools is talking about it with other people.

No One Is Excluded from Pain

The thing about pain is it doesn't have a type. There's no group that's excluded from pain. Pain doesn't care about race, gender, religion, or creed. Pain is universal. No one is immune. Oh, we might not like to admit it, we may go to great lengths to deny it, but we have all experienced pain. People all around you are hurting in ways you may not be able to see and may never know, because there are not always outward signs or signals to alert us to the pain of others.

People may try to hide their pain, or pretend it doesn't exist, but people around you are hurting, even when it doesn't look like it. The truth is every one of us is either coming out of, heading into, or currently dealing with a painful situation. Pain is inevitable. I cannot express to you how much I wish this wasn't true, but it is. We can either deny it, or do something about it.

Most people choose to deny or cover their pain. It feels easier; it feels safer. Many people walk around smiling and looking great on the outside while they are dying on the inside. They don't feel like they can let people know how they are hurting. They might be afraid of being judged or mocked or pushed away. Even in places where people should feel safe to express pain, like our churches, many feel the need to hide and pretend it's all okay.

Jesus came to help people who are hurting. When he walked the earth, he spent most of his time with people who were in pain. Yes, he healed the sick, but he also loved those who were unlovely. He spent his time with tax collectors and sinners. They were outcasts; they weren't the right kinds of people. The religious leaders of his day couldn't understand why Jesus spent time with such people. They asked Jesus' followers why they would want to eat and drink with tax collectors and sinners.

When Jesus overheard their comments he said, "It is not the healthy who need a doctor, but the sick. I have not come to call the righteous, but sinners to repentance" (Luke 5:31–32). Jesus came to help people who were in pain. That's good news for you and me because we are people who have been, or are, sick. It's been said that our churches need to be hospitals for sinners, not hotels for saints. But many don't feel safe expressing their pain at church.

My family attends church on Saturday nights at six o'clock when the "cool" junior high service meets. I know you'll have a hard time believing this, but sometimes we run a little late. There are five of us, and I don't remember the last time we needed to get anywhere when all three kids had their shoes on, wore seasonally appropriate clothes, and had everything they needed to walk out the door on time.

When we run late, my temper can be a little short. I hate being late. I hate rushing. One Saturday I found myself yelling to the kids, "Hurry up and get in the car so we can get to church! And remember, no one knows what a mess we are, so don't blow it!" Even the Celebrate Recovery guy didn't want anyone to know we were having a tough day. I can't blame anyone else for not wanting to stand out.

That means that even the people who look like they have it all together are hurting. The woman who is always put together, with her makeup done and her outfit on point, she's hurting. The man who is in great shape with perfect teeth, he's hurting. The family that looks perfect, with kids that get straight A's every semester and send out beautiful Christmas cards, they are hurting too. It isn't just the guy with the messy hair and stubble. It isn't just the stressed-out woman. It's all of us. Acknowledging that pain in others' lives, and accepting them in their pain, is crucial to understanding and serving them.

Pain Radar

To love others the way Jesus commands us to, we must develop a pain radar. We must start to see people as they really are, not the way they present themselves. I'm not suggesting we dig and dig into people's lives until they finally admit their pain, but we do need to become more aware of their pain. Instead of always saying the casual and meaningless, "How are you doing?" in conversation, we need to stop and listen to people.

We have come up with casual conversations to make interactions easier, but if we don't have an active pain radar we will miss out on cues that can alert us to people's pain. Usually when we're asked how we are doing we will respond with a noncommittal "I'm good" or "Keeping busy," but sometimes our guard slips and some truth is revealed. An active pain radar will key in on these cues and allow us to love and help others.

I wouldn't expect someone I have a casual relationship with to reveal all of their pain to me at once, but there are things to listen for. It might be a simple "I'm so tired lately" or "I'm running around like a crazy person, but I can never seem to get ahead" that cues you into pain. It might be a far-off look or an unwillingness to respond to a text or phone call that tells you all is not well. Maybe it's a heavy sigh in the middle of a conversation or a mention of a worry about something coming up that sets off the alarm bells on your radar. If we key into conversations, if we really listen instead of wait for our turn to talk, we can pick up on the pain going on in other people's lives. Then we can look for ways to help them.

We don't want to expose someone else's pain for our benefit or to gossip about them; we want to serve them. We want to be safe people for them to confide in and point them to the way we found, and are finding, healing from our pain. We want to be able to point them to Jesus. We want to let them know that he cares about their pain, and so do we. We want to let them know they are not alone. We want to be safe people for them. In the next chapter we will go over how serving other people can help our recovery, but that starts with understanding that people are hurting.

So how do you develop a pain radar? It starts with becoming aware. It starts with shifting your perspective and focus from yourself to others. A word of warning is needed here. Many of us, myself included, struggle with codependency. A textbook definition of codependency is hard to come by, and if you ask a hundred codependents what it means to be a codependent, you'll get a hundred different answers. One thing most codependents have in common is a tendency to think of others too much. Codependents tend to put their needs behind the needs of others. They tend to focus more on other people, and less on themselves.

But wait a minute. Isn't that a good thing? Isn't that a *Christian* thing? Earlier in this chapter didn't we look at Philippians 2, "Do nothing out of selfish ambition or vain conceit. Rather, in humility value others above yourselves, not looking to your own interests but each of you to the interests of the others" (Phil. 2:3–4)? Yes, it can be a good thing, it can be a Christian thing, and thinking of others as above ourselves is certainly in the Bible, but there is a major distinction that needs to be made. The difference between codependency and Christian living is: who are you trying to please? If you put others above yourself or serve others so that they will love you more, that's codependency.

However, if you serve others and think more of them than you because you are trying to please Jesus, that is a Christlike way to live.

If we humble ourselves and think of other people, if we place their needs above ours, if we serve them unselfishly out of gratitude for what Jesus has done for us, we are doing it the right way. If we are doing all of those things, but we are doing it for accolades, or so that others notice and love us, or if we do it to please people, we need to be careful. Developing our pain radars starts with becoming aware.

The next step is to slow down enough to listen. This can be so hard. But slow down. Listen to what people say. As I mentioned earlier, it might not be an outright admission of pain, but listen for the cues. Pay attention to people. We live in a busy world with lots of distractions. I used to wear my earbuds pretty much all the time, at least when I was alone. If I was running errands, like grocery shopping or picking up a prescription, I'd have my earbuds in. I love listening to podcasts, audiobooks, and music, but what I was really doing was keeping the world out. It's hard to talk to someone with earbuds in. I was keeping myself distracted and busy. I was also making it impossible to listen to other people.

I've challenged myself to leave my earbuds out of my ears more often. When I go to the store, or when I'm out running errands, I leave my earbuds at home or in the car.

I'm trying to become more aware of people; I'm trying to upgrade my pain radar. If I'm at the gym or if I'm working at a coffee shop, my earbuds are in because they help me focus on the job at hand. But I have found that when they are out, and when my phone is away, I am more engaged with others around me. I have conversations with cashiers that I didn't have before. I talk to people in the stores. At first I was worried people would think I was weird for talking to them, but I am finding that most people are looking for human interaction. Slow down long enough to listen. Be available.

So become aware, slow down and listen, and then be a safe person. This is the last step in developing a pain radar. Be a shelter in the storm for people. When someone confides in you, keep it to yourself. Don't rush in to fix them, but be a safe person that they feel comfortable sharing with. When people learn you are safe, they will confide in you more and more. Often people will share a sliver of their life with you to see if you are safe. When they find you haven't gossiped about them, when you don't laugh at them or judge them, when they find that you are safe, they will go deeper.

One key to being a safe person for other people is not trying to hide your pain from them. When we hide our pain and try to keep a smile on our faces and pretend it's all okay, we keep people from knowing the real us. Now I'm not suggesting that we demonstrate our pain for the entire world to see. You don't need to buy a T-shirt that says, "I'm messed up, ask me how!" But I am suggesting you allow others to see into your life.

A safe person is somehow obvious to people. Perfect strangers will approach someone they identify as safe, perhaps because there is an openness or some subliminal sign that safe people give off. I've seen it happen with my wife. Jeni is one of the safest people I know. She has people confide in her all the time. She'll come home from dropping the kids off at school and tell me a mom she's never met before told her about something going on in her life. She will never tell me what the mom said, just that it happened. I've learned not to ask who it was or what they shared; it's not coming out of Jeni. Somehow, people have learned that Jeni is a safe person to talk to. I'm sure in certain circles people have shared how she has helped them, but I also know that there is something about her that says, "I am safe." In this way being a safe person increases the range of your pain radar. You will begin to seek out those you can serve, and they will begin to know you are safe and reveal themselves to you.

People around you, right now, are hurting. Some of them are in so much pain they don't even know how to express it. Others have recently come out of a painful experience, and some are heading into one. You are not alone. If

ge. You have the courage it takes to examine your life
o something about what you find.

common question I'm asked is, "Johnny, when will I
ne with recovery?" I can answer only for myself. I will
be done with recovery. Remember the onion? I'll keep
ng back layers of my onion and allowing God to work
e and in me to make me look more like Jesus. I have
g way to go. The thing about recovery is at its core,
is a paradox. If we want to keep what we have gained,
ave to give it away. We need to start serving others. So
e are a couple things at work here. First, recovery can
lifelong pursuit because we can always grow closer to
s, and second, giving back to others, or serving, is an
ntial component of recovery.

Serving Is Manditory

ether you check out Celebrate Recovery for a season or
sider yourself a lifer, service is mandatory. To stay on
road to freedom, you have to give your time and talents
ay to others. One way to know we are in recovery is
en we find we are thinking less often about ourselves
d instead are serving others more. Serving others is a key
recovery and leads to deeper healing. God has designed
to need each other and has shaped us to serve others.

Once again, Jesus is the example for us. The night

you are in pain right now, you don't have to go through it
on your own. You can find someone and share what's going
on in your life. You don't have to tell the world, but attend a
Celebrate Recovery group and find someone you can share
with. You might feel like no one will understand you, but
you are wrong. You will find people who know what it's like
to go through pain, because they have gone, or are going
through it too.

If you have been through Celebrate Recovery, if you
have a relationship with Jesus, you have the answer to the
pain around you. It's up to us to reach out and help the
people around us. We need to put our recovery into practice
and help those who are hurting. That's why it's so important
to develop a pain radar. When we see people's pain we can
love them; we can treat them with grace and decency. We
can be the change in the world. When we realize that others
are hurting, we can forgive them when they hurt us. There's
one more thing we can do for them that we will explore in
the next chapter. When we develop a pain radar, we can
serve others well.

Serving others le

deeper healin

In the time I have been fortunate enou
in Celebrate Recovery, I have seen tho
find freedom from all kinds of hurts, hang
I've seen people come into recovery for a
completing a Step Study and then going
church, and I've seen others that refer t
Celebrate Recovery "lifers." A lifer is some
he or she will be in Celebrate Recovery for
lives. One type of person isn't better than t
have been in Celebrate Recovery for any len
found some healing from your issues, you ha

cour
and

be d
neve
peel
on
a lo
ther
we
ther
be
Jes
ess

W
co
th
av
w
a
tc
u

before he was to be turned over to the authorities to be crucified, he showed us the way we should serve others. Jesus gathered his disciples and did something to them that they could not believe. He washed their feet.

This takes a little context. First, feet are disgusting. They are sweaty and smelly. Add to this that the disciples walked everywhere. There were no cars, no buses, no Uber. There were only sandals. That means their feet would get dirty. And Jesus offers to wash these smelly, disgusting feet. He dresses like a servant, taking off his outer robe and tying a towel around his waist. He takes out a bowl of water, scrubs his disciples' feet, and uses the towel around his waist to dry them off. This is definitely a close encounter with Jesus. It was up close and personal.

Then Peter speaks up. He realizes what Jesus is about to do and tells him not to wash his feet. Have I mentioned how much I love Peter? Here he is, thinking he's doing the right thing. He thinks he's being pious by telling Jesus no, and Jesus tells him that unless he washes Peter's feet, Peter won't belong to him. So Peter basically says, "Then give me a bath!" I can picture Jesus patting old Pete on the shoulder and saying, "Calm down, this is an object lesson, just let me wash your feet." Eventually Jesus washes all of the disciples' feet, including Peter's.

Then he asked them, "Do you understand what I have done for you? . . . You call me 'Teacher' and 'Lord,' and rightly so, for that is what I am. Now that I, your Lord and Teacher, have washed your feet, you also should wash one another's feet. I have set you an example that you should do as I have done for you. Very truly I tell you, no servant is greater than his master, nor is a messenger greater than the one who sent him. Now that you know these things, you will be blessed if you do them" (John 13:12–17). Jesus showed us the way to serve others.

Does Jesus mean we are to literally wash each other's feet? Maybe. But I think the lesson is what's important here. When Jesus put on the towel and started washing their feet, he was taking on a lowly position. He was fulfilling one of the lowest jobs of the servants. Jesus could have demanded to be served, but he said, "For even the Son of Man did not come to be served, but to serve, and to give his life as a ransom for many" (Mark 10:45).

He could have come as a king; instead he entered the world as a baby. He could have come in power and thunder, towering above us. Instead, as Paul writes, "[Jesus], being in very nature God, did not consider equality with God something to be used to his own advantage; rather, he made himself nothing by taking the very nature of a servant, being made in human likeness. And being found in appearance as a man, he humbled himself by becoming obedient to death—even death on a cross!" (Phil. 2:6–8). Jesus showed us, over and over again, how to serve one another.

First, we need to humble ourselves. *Humility* has become a dirty word in our culture. I think that's partially due to a core misunderstanding of what humility is. As Pastor John Baker says, humility is not thinking less of yourself; it's thinking of yourself less. People act as if being humble means you have to put yourself down, or that you can never take a compliment or be happy with something you've done. But being humble is simply knowing who, and Whose, you are. As a child of the King you have been given certain gifts. The Bible talks about spiritual gifts that are given to believers, and since you and I are made in the image of God, he has also blessed us with things that mirror and honor him. If you are funny, it's because God has a sense of humor. If you are artistic, it's because God is an artist. If you love others, it is because God is love. Humility isn't saying you don't possess those or other gifts; it's acknowledging that those gifts come from God.

Humility

Humility is also seeing yourself as less important than others. It's all about who you are trying to please. Humbling ourselves means that we don't see ourselves as the most important person in a relationship. When Jeni and I got engaged, a pastor told us a successful marriage is one where both people try to outserve each other. Jeni and I took this to heart and really do try to put each other's needs above our own. Of course we aren't perfect at this! We often get it wrong. In my selfishness and pride it's easy to want to be in charge or important. Not just with Jeni, but in many relationships I often want to get my own way. But it's when I humble myself and put others' needs ahead of my own that I can serve them.

So we need to humble ourselves. That means we don't always look for the most important job. We don't seek to serve people in ways we think are cool; we meet people's needs. Also, notice that Jesus didn't stand up and make a show of getting the water and towel ready. He didn't say, "Okay, disciples, gather round. I'm going to serve you now." He didn't do this in the middle of the courtyard or in front of a bunch of onlookers. No, he gathered them together in private. We can tell from Peter's reaction that Jesus caught them off guard. Yes, he explained what he had done afterward, but he was used to having to explain things to them. After pretty much every lesson he taught, he had to pull them aside and explain the lesson to them. He served them in humility.

Meet People's Needs

After we humble ourselves we need to meet people's needs. That's the simplest way to serve others. Find out what they need and provide it. That might mean giving money or things to people that are in need, but it could also mean giving our time or attention. It could mean listening to someone that needs to vent, or helping someone move. It could mean picking up the phone or picking someone up from the airport. Meeting people's needs means serving them the way they need to be served, not the way we want to serve them.

The Bible says it this way, "Suppose a brother or a sister is without clothes and daily food. If one of you says to them, 'Go in peace; keep warm and well fed,' but does nothing about their physical needs, what good is it?" (James 2:15–16).

Service requires action. Yes, we need to pray for others and ask God to meet their needs, but we also need to know that we may be the answer to that prayer. God may be telling you that you can serve them and meet their needs.

Who Are You Really Serving?

After we humble ourselves and try to meet people's needs, the next thing to do is remember who we are really serving. When we help others we are not just serving them, but we are serving Jesus. Jesus said, "Then the righteous will answer him, 'Lord, when did we see you hungry and feed you, or thirsty and give you something to drink? When did we see you a stranger and invite you in, or needing clothes and clothe you? When did we see you sick or in prison and go to visit you?' The King will reply, 'Truly I tell you, whatever you did for one of the least of these brothers and sisters of mine, you did for me'" (Matt. 25:37–40).

Jesus is telling us we serve him directly when we serve other people. I love this. I love that when I serve other people I am actually serving Jesus. Many times I wish I could give back to Jesus for all that he's given me. I'm not talking about earning my salvation or paying him back, like my service somehow evens the ledger, but simply saying thank you through my actions. As we so often say, actions speak louder than words, and when we serve Jesus by serving others, we are saying thank you with clear action.

Celebrate Recovery has met every Friday night at Saddleback Church in Lake Forest for over twenty-five years. Every Friday night. Now that Saddleback is a multisite campus, meaning we are one church in many locations, Celebrate Recovery meets at different Saddleback campuses throughout the week. These meetings would be impossible without the dozens of volunteers who serve so faithfully. These men and women serve in ways that go unseen by me and the other staff members, but not a moment of their service escapes the notice of Jesus.

They serve by greeting people as they arrive, preparing a meal before the meeting, overseeing share groups, meeting

one-on-one with people, answering the phone, spending time walking through life with newcomers, and so much more. If I listed all the ways these amazing servants give back, I would run out of pages in this book. Celebrate Recovery would not be what it is today without each person who has given so selflessly over the last twenty-five years. Every time they have answered the phone in the middle of the night to talk to someone in the middle of a tough situation and prayed for them, they have done that for Jesus. Every time they set up chairs or picked up trash, they have done that for Jesus. Every bulletin handed out, every hamburger grilled, every small act of kindness has been done for Jesus.

The leaders at Celebrate Recovery all over the world are giving back to others out of what they have been given. They are continuing the cycle of recovery by helping others. They have learned that there is a purpose for their pain and that Jesus cares about their pain. They have done the hard work of facing their past pain and mistakes head on; they have offered forgiveness and made amends when possible. They are aware that the people around them are in pain, and now they are giving back by serving others. That's recovery.

Sobriety versus Recovery

It is possible to be sober and not be in recovery. Sobriety is abstaining from something, be it a substance, a relationship, or a behavior, while recovery is helping others find healing. Recovery is a lifestyle. Recovery requires service. Recovery is all about allowing God to recycle our pain, using it for the benefit of others. Jesus is setting us free from our hurts, hang-ups, and habits, and we are to use that freedom for others. We read in Galatians, "You, my brothers and sisters, were called to be free. But do not use your freedom to indulge the flesh; rather, serve one another humbly in love" (Gal. 5:13). That's what it means to serve other people. We come to recovery for ourselves, but eventually we shift the focus from ourselves to other people. We serve out of the fullness that Christ has given us.

If you are in Celebrate Recovery and you are not yet serving others, what are you waiting for? Get out there and serve! I've already listed a number of ways you can serve at Celebrate Recovery. You don't have to wait until you're invited to serve or you've achieved a certain number of days of sobriety. Just start serving. Look for areas that need attention at your home group, and ask if you can do it. I guarantee you the leaders of your Celebrate Recovery group are looking for people to help. Go to them and ask where you can serve.

But what if you aren't in Celebrate Recovery. Does that mean you're off the hook for serving? No, you're not. Service is a component of faith, a proof of our faith and our love for each other. If you are a follower of Jesus, serving is an you are in pain right now, you don't have to go through it on your own. You can find someone and share what's going on in your life. You don't have to tell the world, but attend a Celebrate Recovery group and find someone you can share with. You might feel like no one will understand you, but you are wrong. You will find people who know what it's like to go through pain, because they have gone, or are going through it too.

If you have been through Celebrate Recovery, if you have a relationship with Jesus, you have the answer to the pain around you. It's up to us to reach out and help the people around us. We need to put our recovery into practice and help those who are hurting. That's why it's so important to develop a pain radar. When we see people's pain we can love them; we can treat them with grace and decency. We can be the change in the world. When we realize that others are hurting, we can forgive them when they hurt us. There's one more thing we can do for them that we will explore in the next chapter. When we develop a pain radar, we can serve others well.

Serving others leads to
deeper healing

In the time I have been fortunate enough to be involved in Celebrate Recovery, I have seen thousands of people find freedom from all kinds of hurts, hang-ups, and habits. I've seen people come into recovery for a season, perhaps completing a Step Study and then going elsewhere in the church, and I've seen others that refer to themselves as Celebrate Recovery "lifers." A lifer is someone who knows he or she will be in Celebrate Recovery for the rest of their lives. One type of person isn't better than the other. If you have been in Celebrate Recovery for any length of time and found some healing from your issues, you have tremendous courage. You have the courage it takes to examine your life and do something about what you find.

A common question I'm asked is, "Johnny, when will I be done with recovery?" I can answer only for myself. I will never be done with recovery. Remember the onion? I'll keep peeling back layers of my onion and allowing God to work on me and in me to make me look more like Jesus. I have a long way to go. The thing about recovery is at its core, there is a paradox. If we want to keep what we have gained, we have to give it away. We need to start serving others. So there are a couple things at work here. First, recovery can be a lifelong pursuit because we can always grow closer to Jesus, and second, giving back to others, or serving, is an essential component of recovery.

Serving Is Manditory

Whether you check out Celebrate Recovery for a season or consider yourself a lifer, service is mandatory. To stay on the road to freedom, you have to give your time and talents away to others. One way to know we are in recovery is when we find we are thinking less often about ourselves and instead are serving others more. Serving others is a key to recovery and leads to deeper healing. God has designed us to need each other and has shaped us to serve others.

Once again, Jesus is the example for us. The night

essential component of your faith. Again, serving doesn't earn your salvation, but it does show you are saved.

Serving is so against our culture. We live in a me-first world. With the rise of social media, we are more and more focused on ourselves and promoting an image we want the world to see. I'm not saying social media is evil; it isn't. It's just a tool, but just as any tool can be misused to become a weapon, so can social media. We spend so much time checking our timelines, looking for likes or shares, seeing who is following us, and presenting a picture to the world of how we want to be seen that the focus is completely on us.

The other day I took a picture of my son and me hanging out and posted it on social media. After a few minutes I checked to see how many likes it had gotten. Jimmy looked over my shoulder and was disappointed that it hadn't garnered the number of likes he had hoped for. I took time away from spending time with my son to show the world that I was spending time with my son. Then I took more time to check to see if you liked it.

Is that evil? No. Was it wrong for me to post a picture of our "dude day"? I don't think so. But I also don't think it was necessary or the best use of that time together. I certainly didn't need to model the behavior of checking to see if the post had gotten attention. We are so focused on ourselves it is almost impossible to focus on other people. Remember, people around us are in pain. As we develop our pain radars, we will notice their pain more and more. When we take the focus off of ourselves and serve others, we are going against the grain of what our culture is becoming.

So how can we serve others more effectively? How can we give back what we've gotten? What I have learned through Celebrate Recovery is that there are as many ways to serve as there are people. Here are some ways that we can begin to serve others, right now.

Ways to Serve

First, give back what you have been given. "Each of you should use whatever gift you have received to serve others, as faithful stewards of God's grace in its various forms" (1 Peter 4:10). Again, this is what Celebrate Recovery is all about. We give back out of what Jesus has done for us. It all starts here, with the cycle of service. Someone comes to Celebrate Recovery and finds freedom and healing from a hurt, hang-up, or habit. While they are in Celebrate Recovery other people are serving them, helping them along the way. They begin to serve others out of the victory and comfort they are finding. The cycle continues.

One of the theme verses for Celebrate Recovery is "Praise be to the God and Father of our Lord Jesus Christ, the Father of compassion and the God of all comfort, who comforts us in all our troubles, so that we can comfort those in any trouble with the comfort we ourselves receive from God" (2 Cor. 1:3–4). God comforts us, not only for ourselves, but for other people as well. So we give back out of what we have been given.

The best present is your presence. The absolute best way to serve other people is by being available. There is nothing that will replace your presence. I'm still in the lucky phase where my kids want to hang out with me. I know this won't last forever, but for now, they like being with me. If I'm running an errand, or doing something around the house, they want to be with me. Sometimes, I want to be alone. At heart I am an introvert, and times of quiet and isolation can recharge me. But isolation is a tricky thing. Too much is bad for me, and I have to fight against isolating all the time. When I'm running an errand and one of my kids wants to come with me, I have to choose between my alone time and time with my children, whom I love. I have gotten better and better at this. I travel frequently and I know I need to spend time with them now, while they still want to. But if I am with them and I'm constantly looking at my phone, checking email and answering texts, am I really with them?

I love and use gadgets and tech all the time. I'm active on social media and love that there are ways to connect with people from all over the world. But, in my own life, and in the lives of many of us, social media and technology are robbing others of our time and attention. We can serve others by giving them our attention. When someone I love gives me their attention, they are showing me they love me. When someone I admire gives me their attention, I am filled with the feeling that I am important to them.

Have you ever run into an old friend that you haven't seen in a while and said, "We should get lunch sometime," knowing that neither of you were going to follow up on it? It happens all the time. It's polite. It's friendly. It's empty. Both people walk away feeling good that they made an effort and feel completely sure that they won't actually have to go to lunch with that person. But what if, the next time that happened, you got out your phone and made an appointment to get together? What if you didn't cancel it before you actually got together? That would communicate that you actually cared about that person. It would show, not say that you would like to get together with them and catch up. It would be unexpected. It would be serving them with your attention.

"I'll Pray for You"

There's a Christian version of "we should get lunch sometime" and it's "I'll pray for you." Praying for other people is great, but I have found, at least in my own life, that when I say I'll pray for someone I don't always actually pray for that person. A while ago a friend I deeply admire changed the way I think about this. While I was talking about some issues I was going through she listened and said, "Can I pray for you about this?" And right there, she prayed for me. She served me in that moment with her prayer and with her attention. You and I can serve others with our presence.

Another way to serve others is by mentoring, or what Celebrate Recovery would call sponsoring. Mentoring is simply guiding someone down the road you have traveled. You don't have to have it all together; my best mentors have always been great at admitting their shortcomings. You just have to be ahead of the other person on your journey. In Celebrate Recovery we call our mentors *sponsors*. They are people who are ahead of us in recovery and who serve as guides for us.

Sponsors can help make sure we are going through the Recovery Principles at the right pace. If we are going too slowly, they can encourage us to pick up the pace. However, if we are going too fast, they can help us slow down. Sponsors serve by giving back. They serve as sounding boards and help us apply recovery principles to our lives. If you have been in recovery for a while, and by a while I mean over a year or two, and you have not yet sponsored anyone, I'd encourage you to open yourself up to the experience. Let people know you are available. Then give back what you have been given.

I'll never forget a conversation I had with my first sponsor. Bob was well ahead of me on the road to recovery, and he was a great sponsor in my early days. One day Jeni and I had been in an argument over something silly. I know it was silly because I can't remember what it was about. The important thing was, I was right. I knew it in my bones. I was right and she was wrong. Oh, she thought it was the other way around, but *I was right*! I spent about an hour on the phone with Bob detailing all the ways I was right, and maybe more importantly how she was wrong, and Bob patiently listened. Finally he said, "Johnny, do you want to be right or well?" I answered, "Can't I be both?" He chuckled and said, "Let me rephrase that, do you want to be right or married?" We had a good laugh and we talked about how the important thing in this disagreement was that I needed to relent and apologize. I might have been right (I so was), but I was wrong in the way I was handling it. Bob helped me see the situation in a different light. He guided me down the path.

If you are new to Celebrate Recovery, you can still help others by being an accountability partner. If sponsors are our guides, then accountability partners are fellow travelers. They are people who are on the road to recovery alongside us. While you typically have only one sponsor at a time, you can, and should, have multiple accountability partners. Accountability partners actually serve each other at the same time. It's a two-way street. No matter where you are in your recovery journey, you can serve others by being available in this way.

A quick note about sponsors and accountability partners: for your safety and theirs, they should be the same gender as yourself. Accountability partners and sponsors end up spending a lot of time together on the phone and in person. While I have female friends and have learned a lot from women in recovery, I don't have these kinds of relationships with them. There is much to say on this, but just know that many dangers can be avoided if you follow the simple guideline of keeping your sponsors and accountability partners gender specific.

With that in mind, accountability partners are available for us when we are hurting or when we need help. Not everyone in your life will understand or support what you are doing in Celebrate Recovery. Some will prefer that you stay just where you are because your change puts a spotlight on their own hurts, hang-ups, and habits. When that happens, accountability partners can help keep us encouraged and on the right path. They are people we can reach out to before we go back to an old behavior. They can give us the pat on the back we need to keep going. These relationships don't need to be formalized. I have lots of accountability partners who probably don't even know I call them that. They just think we are friends. And we *are* friends; that's the point. They are men I rely on to help me along the journey, and I hope that I help them as well.

There is no reason to wait to start serving people. The

time to start serving others is now! So far we've looked at what serving does for other people, but there is one more benefit to service: it is a key to lasting change. Yes, our focus on serving needs to be helping others, but serving others also leads to our growth. We've already explored how serving others takes the focus off of us and puts it on them, and that is one reason it is so important. But serving others also helps us in two important ways: it reminds us of where we have been, and it makes us put our recovery into practice.

I love spending time with the newcomer. I love spending time talking to people who are brand new to Celebrate Recovery. People don't usually attend Celebrate Recovery for the first time on a great day, a day they get a promotion, get engaged, or get some really good news. They usually come on the day they get fired, get separated, or get some really bad news. This isn't always the case, but it is usually how it works.

So when someone walks in the doors of Celebrate Recovery for the first time, they are usually in pain. They are nervous; they aren't sure they are in the right place. I love spending time with these newcomers to calm them down and assure them they are safe. I like to hear about what they are going through and try to point them in the right direction. I like doing this for them, but I also like doing it for me. Hearing the newcomer's story reminds me of where I was when I began Celebrate Recovery. It reminds me of the pain I was experiencing and how I never want to go back there. As a result it encourages me to keep my guard up and keep moving forward.

If you have ever watched a boxing match or a mixed martial arts fight, you have probably noticed the coaches in the corners. They shout instructions to the fighters in the ring and help them see what their opponent is doing. One thing you'll hear often is, "Keep your hands up!" The coaches are reminding the fighters of the first rule of fighting: don't let the other guy hit you. Spending time with newcomers reminds me to keep my hands up. It helps me identify areas where I've made compromises or relaxed too much so that I am now at risk of either relapse or acting out on a different issue. Meeting with a newcomer, and serving them, is primarily about them, but it can also strengthen and protect my recovery as well.

It also helps me put my recovery into practice. The Eighth Principle of Celebrate Recovery says that I "yield myself to be used by God, both in my example and in my words." Serving others allows me to actually do this principle. I don't want to be all talk; I want to back it up with action. Yielding ourselves means that we allow God to use us, opening ourselves up to God like the prophet Isaiah, who said, "Then I heard the voice of the Lord saying, 'Whom shall I send? And who will go for us?' And I said, 'Here am I. Send me!'" (Isa. 6:8). People are hurting, and

God wants to use other people to help them. He wants to use *you* to help them. God wants to take what he has done in your life and replicate it in someone else's.

We find so many blessings in serving other people. When we serve others, we not only serve them directly, but we also serve Jesus and strengthen our own recovery in the meantime. That seems like a pretty good deal to me.

There's no one God doesn't love, won't forgive, or can't change

Yesterday was a tough day. Over the course of writing this book I've had a lot of ups and downs. Yesterday was pretty much full of downs. It all centered on one question I could not shake. I kept asking myself the same question over and over: "Who do you think you are?"

I have spent most of the time writing this book at coffee shops or at my kitchen table late at night when my family is asleep. While it isn't my first writing project, it's the first thing I'm writing on my own. I've had a few moments during this process that I've felt like deleting the whole thing, calling my publisher, and telling them I couldn't do it.

Yesterday as I finished writing I honestly really began to struggle. I started thinking about all the ways I have blown it in the past, and all the mistakes I make even today, and over and over again I kept saying to myself, "No, really! Who do you think you are?" At times the process of writing this book has been amazing and helped me understand the things I've learned in Celebrate Recovery about myself, other people, and, most importantly, Jesus. At other times it has felt overwhelming. Because, who do I think I am?

"Who Do I Think I Am?"

I'll tell you who I am: I'm Johnny, a believer in Jesus Christ who struggles. I struggle with alcoholism, codependency, anxiety, and much more. I am a broken, imperfect person who, on his own merits, is not qualified to write this or any other book. I am a sinner. But I am also a child of God, and that title pretty much makes the rest of that stuff irrelevant. I battle with the feeling that I am not a good enough person to be a pastor, or a writer, or a leader in Celebrate Recovery. On my own, I am not good enough. On my own my brokenness and my sinfulness disqualify me from this kind of service. Thankfully, though, I am not on my own!

Our pain has a purpose. I think I went through yesterday's pain so I could write what I need to today. I think God was doing a few things for me yesterday. First, he was reminding me that I am utterly dependent on him. Sometimes I forget that. I'll start to feel proud of myself or wander back into the desire to earn his love and he will gently correct me. The Bible says, "The Lord disciplines those he loves, as a father the son he delights in" (Prov. 3:12).

God disciplines us because we are his children and he loves us. I've written a lot about my kids because they are daily reminders for me about God. I hate disciplining my kids, but I do it because I love them and want them to learn from me. I want to help them make good choices, and to do that I have to discipline them when they make bad ones. Yesterday, God was gently disciplining me, guiding me back to dependence on him. Look at what Paul said about this: "It does not, therefore, depend on human desire or effort, but on God's mercy" (Rom. 9:16). When I forget this God nudges me back. I was focusing on who I am without Jesus, but I am never without Jesus. When I asked, "Who do you think you are?" God was responding, "You are my child."

God was reminding me that who I was is not who I am becoming. I have made huge mistakes, and yesterday I was focusing on those mistakes. I was dredging up those past mistakes not to deal with them but to punish myself with them. When Paul was struggling with these kinds of issues, he said, "But one thing I do: Forgetting what is behind and straining toward what is ahead, I press on toward the goal to win the prize for which God has called me heavenward in Christ Jesus" (Phil. 3:13–14).

If we have done the work of dealing with our past mistakes, and I have, we need to move forward. God reminded me of that this morning. I was beating myself up and allowing those mistakes to keep me stuck. When I asked, "Who do you think you are?" God responded, "My child, you are changing."

Another thing I think God was reminding me of yesterday is that he loves me. I believe God allows me to go through times like that so he can remind me of how much he loves me. We read in Ephesians, "And I pray that you, being rooted and established in love, may have power, together with all the Lord's holy people, to grasp how wide and long and high and deep is the love of Christ, and to know this love that surpasses knowledge—that you may be filled to the measure of all the fullness of God" (Eph. 3:17–19). God loves me in ways I cannot fully grasp, but the prayer in Ephesians is that I will someday understand it. When I was asking, "Who do you think you are?" God was responding, "You are loved."

The last thing I think God wanted to remind me of yesterday is that you might be feeling this way too. You may be feeling like you are disqualified or unworthy or unlovable. You might be going through something just like this, or it may be a feeling you have pretty much all of the time. I think it's a normal condition for people to experience at least periodically. You may be on the cusp of a breakthrough in your recovery, victory and freedom might be right within your reach, and you might think, "Who do I think I am? Do I really think I can change?"

You might have found some freedom in your life and now you're considering serving others. You might be stepping up into leadership at your Celebrate Recovery, becoming a sponsor or accountability partner, or have a desire to somehow help others find what you have found. If you're in this place you might think, "Who do I think I am? Do I really think I can help others?"

You might be finally ready to check out Celebrate Recovery for the very first time. You may have identified your hurts, hang-ups, and habits, and you're finally ready to bring those things to Jesus and ask him to help you. You might be thinking, "Who do I think I am? Can I really find freedom?"

You might be beating yourself up over past mistakes and failures, running them over and over again in your mind. You may lie awake at night playing the tapes in your mind of the things you have done, the actions you have taken, and feel worse and worse about yourself as they play. You might be thinking, "Who do I think I am? Can I really be forgiven?"

Or you might have read about Jesus and how he loves you, and you are ready to begin a relationship with him. You are tired of trying to do all of this on your own limited power, and you are ready to rely on his unlimited power.

You might be thinking, "Who do I think I am? Can Jesus really love me?"

If you find yourself in any of these situations, you need to know that Jesus is saying, "Yes!" You can be changed, you can be used, you can be forgiven, and you are loved! There is not a single person in the world that God doesn't love, won't forgive, or can't change. I've seen it in my life and in the lives of countless people around the world. No matter how you might feel about yourself, it doesn't change the fact that God loves you, right now, exactly as you are.

The Most Important Lesson

This is the last Life Lesson because it is the most important. It is the bookend to Life Lesson 1. When we admit we are in pain, that we've made mistakes, that we have issues that need God's help, we find a loving God who accepts us as we are. We find a forgiving God who cleanses us from our sin, and we find a powerful God who makes us new and makes us more like Christ.

God accepts you as you are, but he loves you too much to leave you there.

God Loves You, Just as You Are

A few chapters back, we looked at John 3:16 and Romans 5:8. These two verses are intertwined. God so loves you that he sent Jesus to die for you, that as long as you believe in him you won't die, but you'll find everlasting life (John 3:16). He did that for you before you got your act together, while you were still a sinner (Rom. 5:8).

Jesus' death split history. It doesn't matter if historians want to use BC and AD or BCE and CE, the distinction is Jesus. Jesus' death, burial, and resurrection changed everything! Jesus died over two thousand years ago. None of us were born then. Our parents weren't, and even our great-great-great-grandparents weren't. Jesus died thousands of years before we were born. That means that his death covered our sins that we hadn't even had the chance to commit yet! God did this for you before you heard his name, before you could react to his love, before you could get your act together. God loves you just as you are.

He didn't, and he doesn't, wait for us to get it all together before we come to him; he just invites us to relationship with him. Jesus says, "Here I am! I stand at the door and knock. If anyone hears my voice and opens the door, I will come in and eat with that person, and they with me" (Rev. 3:20). He doesn't say, "I stand at the door and knock. If anyone hears my voice and cleans up their house so it is pretty inside and gets out their fancy china and silverware and puts on their best clothes, I'll think about coming in and having a meal." He stands at the door and knocks, and all we do is open the door and let him in. He loves you just as you are.

But He Loves You Too Much to Let You Stay That Way

When we come to Jesus with our hurts, hang-ups, and habits, he loves and accepts us just as we are, but he also wants to help us get rid of our hurts, hang-ups, and habits. He died for our sins so that we could be free of them, not so we could stay stuck in them. God is holy, meaning he is set apart. He is different. He is perfect. When we accept Jesus' work on the cross, God no longer sees our sin but instead views us as perfect in Jesus. We begin the process of becoming free from our sinful lives. I wish it was as simple as believing and then never struggling with sin again, but the Bible doesn't teach us that.

Many people read 2 Corinthians 5:17, "Therefore, if anyone is in Christ, the new creation has come: The old has gone, the new is here," and determine that they are now so new all of the work is done. They are partly right. The work of the cross is done. We can't do anything to replace what Jesus did for us. No matter how good we are or how hard we work, until we accept Jesus and his sacrifice for us, we will never earn forgiveness or new life.

However, it is wrong to believe that once we accept Jesus there is nothing for us to do. Although God decides to see Jesus' perfection in us, we are still instructed over and over in Scripture to become more like Jesus. When we accept Jesus we become justified, right with God, and then we begin the process of being sanctified, becoming more like Jesus. Jesus said, "Remain in me, as I also remain in you. No branch can bear fruit by itself; it must remain in the vine. Neither can you bear fruit unless you remain in me. I am the vine; you are the branches. If you remain in me and I in you, you will bear much fruit; apart from me you can do nothing" (John 15:4–5).

One thing we do in the sanctification process is to remain in relationship with Jesus. In my life this is harder to remember than it should be. I can get so caught up in my abilities, or feel so self-assured or proud, that I forget to remain in Jesus. And then I wonder why I have so many ups and downs! We must remain in Jesus. By remaining in him we become more like him.

Just as God is holy, we are called to be holy as well; our desire is to become more like him. We don't turn to God in repentance so we can keep sinning. We are told, "For God did not call us to be impure, but to live a holy life" (1 Thess. 4:7). And remember Galatians 5:13, "You, my brothers and sisters, were called to be free. But do not use your freedom to indulge the flesh; rather, serve one another humbly in love."

God's Word is full of instructions that we need to turn from our old ways and follow him. A great picture of what it looks like when we know the way we should go but decide to return to our sinful lives is found in Proverbs: "As a dog returns to its vomit, so fools repeat their folly" (Prov. 26:11). God loves you just where you are, but he loves you too much to let you stay there.

What Is Our Response?

So what's our response? How do we become more like Jesus? Well, I've got some good news: Celebrate Recovery is a sanctification process. When we go through Christ-centered recovery, we become more like Jesus. We admit we need God's power, we remain in him as we travel down the road to recovery and freedom, and we allow him to peel back the layers of the onion to help us become holy. We don't often talk about Celebrate Recovery this way, but it's true.

Hebrews 12:1–3 says, "Therefore, since we are surrounded by such a great cloud of witnesses, let us throw off everything that hinders and the sin that so easily entangles. And let us run with perseverance the race marked out for us, fixing our eyes on Jesus, the pioneer and perfecter of faith. For the joy set before him he endured the cross, scorning its shame, and sat down at the right hand of the throne of God. Consider him who endured such opposition from sinners, so that you will not grow weary and lose heart." Celebrate Recovery helps us throw off everything that hinders us, and it deals directly with the sin that entangles us. It gives us a process to follow to become more like Christ.

You may not feel like God loves you. You might not feel worthy of his love. Fortunately, how we feel about ourselves doesn't change the way God feels about us. The Bible says, "And so we know and rely on the love God has for us. God is love. Whoever lives in love lives in God, and God in them" (1 John 4:16). God loves you. He loves you deeper than you will ever know. He loves you with a perfect richness that we catch glimpses of in the way we love other people.

Have you ever loved someone so much it hurt? Have you ever looked at someone you loved and wanted to help end their suffering? Have you ever loved someone so much that you were willing to sacrifice for them, maybe even die for them? If so, that's because you are an image of God, and that is how much he loves you. But his love for you is even stronger. His love for you is even more intense. God loves you, right now, just as you are, but he wants to make you more like Jesus. He wants to strip away the things that cause you pain and that keep you from having a deeper relationship with him.

God wants to forgive you. It's tempting to look at your life and think that you are beyond God's forgiveness, but you aren't. This is especially true if you are a follower of Jesus who continues to blow it. Living a sinless life is impossible. The only person to ever do it was Jesus, and he is God in the flesh! You and I will make mistakes. However, when we do, it is easy to feel ashamed and allow that shame to drive a wedge between us and God.

We've already seen that we should run to God and not away from him when we blow it, but it's so important to keep in mind. You are going to make mistakes. So will I. I love the apostle Paul. He understood the struggle so well, because he lived it. He said, "As it is, it is no longer I myself who do it, but it is sin living in me. For I know that good itself does not dwell in me, that is, in my sinful nature. For I have the desire to do what is good, but I cannot carry it out. For I do not do the good I want to do, but the evil I do not want to do—this I keep on doing" (Rom. 7:17–19). Many of us can relate to this so well. Here we are, full of the knowledge of how we should live, but we continue to make bad choices. As we continue down the road to recovery we begin making better and better choices, but we have to acknowledge the struggle.

This is one reason why those of us in Celebrate Recovery identify ourselves as "believers who struggle with (fill in the blank)." It isn't because we haven't found, or are finding, freedom, but because this sinful nature is still within us. It is a struggle. Elsewhere Paul writes, "So I say, walk by the Spirit, and you will not gratify the desires of the flesh. For the flesh desires what is contrary to the Spirit, and the Spirit what is contrary to the flesh. They are in conflict with each other, so that you are not to do whatever you want" (Gal. 5:16–17).

Flesh versus Spirit

There is a battle waging inside each of us between our flesh, or our sinful nature, and the Spirit, which is God living in us. They are in conflict with each other, and it is up to us to decide which one to gratify. Thankfully, Paul also says, "Therefore, there is now no condemnation for those who are in Christ Jesus, because through Christ Jesus the law of the Spirit who gives life has set you free from the law of sin and death" (Rom. 8:1–2).

Jesus has provided a way for us to be forgiven for our sins. *He* is that way. God sent Jesus to forgive us because he loves us. Nowhere in the Bible does it say that Jesus forgives only certain sins. As far as I can see, there is only one unforgivable sin, what Jesus calls "blasphemy against the Spirit" in Matthew 12:31. Commentators describe this as an unwillingness to turn our lives over to Jesus. It's the pride that says we don't need him. It's unbelief in Christ. If we die without turning to him, we are saying we are God and we don't need him; this is blasphemy. Other than unbelief, there is no unforgivable sin. It doesn't matter what you've done, God can forgive you, if you turn to him and accept the work of Jesus on the cross. Does that seem too simple? Does it seem like there should be more to it? If there was, it would make Jesus' sacrifice unnecessary and empty. Jesus died for you and me. He died to forgive us for our sins and make us right with God.

I want to be clear about something: just because we are forgiven for our sins does not mean that sins have no consequences. Sometimes I try to explain this to my kids. They know the house rules. They break a rule, they get caught, they get punished, they say they are sorry for breaking the rule, and the punishment is still enforced.

"But I said I'm sorry!" they say.

"I know, and I forgive you," I say, "but you still have a consequence."

This is almost always followed up with the anthem of children everywhere, "But that's not fair!" To which I reply, "No one said life was fair." I have become my parents. The truth is, having a punishment, or a consequence, for our actions is fair. Say I was speeding down the highway and I was pulled over.

"Sir, do you know why I pulled you over?"

"I guess I might have been speeding just a little bit?"

"Sir, you were going eighty-five in a fifty-five mile per hour zone. License and registration, please."

"Officer, I am so sorry, I didn't realize I was speeding. I'll be more careful."

"Great, license and registration please."

That ticket is coming my way. There was a rule, and I broke it. The police officer might forgive me, but the consequence is coming my way. I'm going to have to pay for that ticket. When we turn to Jesus we find forgiveness, but we cannot expect to escape all of the consequences our sins may have caused.

Drinking too much can damage the liver. When someone

begins recovery and finds sobriety and freedom from their sin addiction to alcohol, they are forgiven for their actions, but the damage to their liver is not immediately reversed.

In our addictions we cause damage to relationships that doesn't disappear just because we have been attending Celebrate Recovery. Those relationships can be healed, if both people commit to the healing process, but it doesn't just happen. There are consequences. God's forgiveness for us is immediate, but those we have hurt may take more time to forgive us. We need to give them the time they need and not demand they forgive us. Just as forgiving those that have hurt us is a process, so it is a process for those we have hurt.

Debts from using credit cards will need to be dealt with and paid. Amends will need to be made. It doesn't mean that you are not forgiven, but Christ's forgiveness does not wipe out any of the consequences our actions made in free will have caused.

That doesn't mean you are alone to face them or that you can never change. Just as God loves you and forgives you, he also has the power to change you.

There Is No Power Greater Than God

Some people compare themselves with others and feel like no one has ever been as bad as they have been. They look at their lives and see only the mistakes they have made, the bad things they have done. They think God might love them, he might even forgive them, but they are doomed to be stuck in their sin. This mindset shows a fundamental misunderstanding of who God is and what his power is capable of. There is no power greater than God. There has never been anything, other than God, powerful enough to speak creation into existence. Read the creation account in Genesis 1. God simply spoke and created the universe. Try that out. Try to speak a sandwich into existence. I'll give you a minute. Look at your hand and say, "Let there be sandwich." Did it work?

Not only did God have the power to create, he also had the power to raise Jesus from the grave. Jesus was laid in the tomb, and after three days he was raised to life again, and not only that, he still lives today, thousands of years later. God showed off his power by raising Jesus back to life. In a moment he said, "Watch this!" And the tomb was empty.

This same power is available to you to help you change. As Paul writes, "And if the Spirit of him who raised Jesus from the dead is living in you, he who raised Christ from the dead will also give life to your mortal bodies because of his Spirit who lives in you" (Rom. 8:11). The power that raised Christ from the grave is inside of you! The same power! If you have trusted Jesus Christ, you have the power to change! Let that sink in. Have you ever found yourself in the cycle of making the same mistake over and over and feeling like you'd never overcome it? With Christ's power, you can! Our own power is so limited that we are easily frustrated when we try to change on our own. We can feel like we will never change. But with God we can.

I have seen, in my life and in the life of those around me, tremendous change and growth. I have seen relationships restored that seemed broken beyond repair. I have seen what appeared to be hopeless addicts find freedom they never thought possible. I have seen people completely change, right in front of my eyes, over time. I have seen spenders become savers. I have seen people break out of isolation and become part of a group. I have seen angry people become friendly and open. I have seen men in prison who have become free of the things that brought them there. I have seen changes you wouldn't believe, including changes in my own life that make the old me unrecognizable to the man I am becoming now.

This power is available to you as well. There has never been a person God doesn't love, won't forgive, or can't change. Including you. All you have to do is accept his love. As Jesus stands knocking at the door of your heart, all you have to do is let him in. Let his love wash over you. When you ask yourself, "Who do you think you are?" answer, "I am loved by God!"

Jesus has already paid for your sins on the cross. No

matter if you are a new believer in Jesus or if you have followed him for years, this forgiveness covers your sins. The Bible says, "He himself bore our sins in his body on the cross, so that we might die to sins and live for righteousness; and by his wounds you have been healed" (1 Peter 2:24). When you are tempted to dredge up the past, not to examine it and deal with it but to torture yourself with it, and you ask yourself, "Who do you think you are?" answer, "I am forgiven."

Jesus has the power to change you. The power that raised him from the grave lives in you to help you overcome any hurt, hang-up, or habit. There is no wound that God can not heal. Instead of leaning on your own power, turn to Jesus and ask for his power. Jesus promises, "Ask and it will be given to you; seek and you will find; knock and the door will be opened to you" (Matt. 7:7). Ask Jesus for his power, and you will find freedom you have never imagined! When you ask yourself, "Who do you think you are?" answer, "I am changing, and God is not done with me yet!"

When you forget how much God loves you, when you are reminded of your past mistakes and feel like God will not forgive you, and when you are tempted to feel like you will never change, remember these words: "For you created my inmost being; you knit me together in my mother's womb. I praise you because I am fearfully and wonderfully made; your works are wonderful, I know that full well. My frame was not hidden from you when I was made in the secret place, when I was woven together in the depths of the earth. Your eyes saw my unformed body; all the days ordained for me were written in your book before one of them came to be" (Ps. 139:13–16).

No matter who you are, what you've done, or what's been done to you, God loves you. And he hasn't left you alone. You have a family that wants to help you on your journey. You need them and they need you.

Conclusion

A few months ago, my family and I moved out of the home we had lived in for more than ten years. We had to do a lot of work on the house to get it ready to sell. We had to fix some drywall that had been removed during one of the leaks. My son's room was one color, my daughters' room was another, and the master was a third. There were weeds in the back yard that we never could pull up all the way. None of these things bothered us. We had lived in the house for a long time and all of those things needed fixing while we lived there, but we weren't motivated to do any of the work. It was okay with us; we were used to it. We didn't even notice most of the problems until we found our new house.

We had been saving and dreaming about being able to move into a slightly bigger house where each kid could have their own room. My girls had been sharing a room since Jimmy was born, and the house was getting pretty tight for the five of us. So when we found our new house, we got super motivated to sell the old one.

All of a sudden, all of the work we had been putting off was crucial to get done. We had plumbers, cleaners, gardeners, and all kinds of handymen out to get it ready to sell. We noticed every crack, every flaw, every little detail we had been overlooking for a decade. We wanted it fixed, and we wanted it fixed now! We painted the whole thing, inside and out, fixed all the leaks, deep cleaned the carpet, and weeded and replanted the back yard.

I remember showing the house and having our realtor give us notes on what potential buyers thought of the place. When they saw things about the house they didn't like, I got super defensive. Sure it's small, but it's cozy. Okay, the kitchen is so tight only one person can be in it at a time, but that allows for some alone time. Yes, the neighbors are close. What, you don't like people? All of these things were complaints I had made over the years, many of them so often my friends and family were tired of hearing it. But now it was different.

While we were closing escrow, I made lots of trips to the now empty house to check on things and drop things off. The last time I went by to drop off the keys, I was suddenly struck by the idea that this was no longer my home. For ten years it had been our home, but now it belonged to someone else. It was different. I was a little sad for a while. I mean, we brought home two of our kids to that house. We had battled croup, bandaged knees, cuddled and hugged and laughed in that house. Now it was something else. It wasn't mine.

When I got to the car I called Jeni and told her I was nostalgic for the old place. We talked about some memories we had there and then she said, "Come home." I drove to our new home, and immediately my melancholy dissipated. I saw our new home and laughed out loud. I was *home*. This house isn't that much bigger. It isn't in a fancy neighborhood or anything you'd see in a home magazine, but we love it. If I walked you through all of the things God lined up for this move to be possible, you'd be blown away. This house is better in pretty much every way. I don't say that to brag; it's just true. There were good memories and bad memories in the old place, and there will be good and bad times here too, but I wouldn't move back to the old house if you paid me to.

"Do You Ever Miss the Old Days?"

A few days ago I was playing catch with my son in the cul-de-sac our house is on. When I get home from work, I have to have my hands free because as soon as my son Jimmy hears my car, he's going to grab his football and throw it at me. I mean *to* me. We love throwing the ball around and talking. It's one of our favorite things to do together. While we were tossing the ball around, I thought about a question a friend had asked me earlier that day. Referring to my days of drinking, he said, "Do you ever miss the old days?" I stopped for a second, caught a little off guard. Then I looked at him and said, "Not even a little." When Jimmy threw the next pass to me I said a little prayer, thanking God for rescuing me from the "good old days" and for bringing me into these new ones.

My old house is sort of like the process of recovery. There are things in our lives that we know need to be dealt with. Some of the hurts, hang-ups, and habits in our lives have been a part of us for years. From time to time, an emergency might point out a problem, but when the crisis passes, we can return to our state of ignorance. Eventually something will happen that will cause us to take a close look at our issues and finally take the steps we need to take to do something about them. Unfortunately, that something is usually a painful experience. It isn't always something painful—people have decided to face their issues for all kinds of reasons—but it hasn't earned the name "rock bottom" for nothing.

When someone hits a rock bottom, they know it is time to act, because the pain has finally gotten worse than the fear of change. Rock bottoms can look different for different people. For some it is another DUI. For others it's a bill they can't hope to pay. For some it's a number on a scale, either one that's too big or too small. Some look at their relationships and can't deny that they are falling apart. Some have gotten medical reports that are too scary to ignore.

Not every rock bottom is dramatic. They can be small moments that get us moving. My moment was knowing that because of my DUI, I couldn't drive Jeni to the hospital when she went into labor with Maggie. That was the beginning of my coming out of denial. Whatever the catalyst, something changes that forces us to take action.

If it hasn't happened for you yet, it will. My prayer for you is that it will be a small spark instead of a forest fire that gets you moving. Maybe it will even be this book. Maybe you've been reading this because someone has been bugging you to and you just want them off your back. That person loves you very much. They want you to find what they have found. They know you have issues, and they want you to experience the freedom from your hurts, hang-ups, and habits that they have found. If that's the case, I hope you'll take a look at your life and see if there's anything out of whack. Maybe take a second and pray the words of David from Psalm 139, "Search me, God, and know my heart; test me and know my anxious thoughts. See if there is any offensive way in me, and lead me in the way everlasting" (Ps. 139:23–24). If God points anything out, take action. Remember, God will use pain to get your attention. You can either pay attention now, or you can wait until it gets worse. I'm praying you pay attention now.

Next Steps

If you find that you have an issue in your life that needs to be dealt with, I encourage you to check out a Celebrate Recovery group in your area. The worst thing you can do is try to fix your issues on your own. Well, actually, the worst thing you can do is continue to ignore them; the *second* worst thing you can do is try to fix it alone. I know it's tempting to look at a big issue in your life and keep it to yourself, but remember, you are as sick as your secrets. Go to www.celebraterecovery.com and go to the "How do I find a Celebrate Recovery" tab. Look for a church in your area that has Celebrate Recovery and then go. You'll find people who want to help you along your road to freedom. They won't try to fix you or judge you. They won't offer you a simple fix, but they will show you the way. Tell them I sent you.

If you've been in Celebrate Recovery for a while, I hope that one or more of these lessons helped you in some way. I know none of them are revolutionary or new, but they are ten of the things I have learned in my time in Celebrate Recovery. I fully intend to keep learning because I am nowhere near done with recovery. I am a lifer, and I hope you are too. I hope that you'll keep letting God work on you while you help others in their journey. I hope you'll offer yourself as "a living sacrifice, holy and pleasing to

God—this is your true and proper worship" (Rom. 12:1). My prayer for you is that you will keep allowing God to peel back the layers of your onion and that you will help comfort others with the comfort you have found. We need men and women like you who are willing to recycle their pain to help others who are hurting.

There are lots of things you can do next, but I'll leave you with this one thing: take the next step you need to take. That will be different for everyone reading this, but I'd guess you know yours. It might be to call a friend and let them know what's going on. It might be to tell someone you aren't going to help hide their secret anymore. It might be time to face your past, make amends, or offer forgiveness. It might be to develop a pain radar and start looking for people to serve. It might be to get off the sidelines and step into service. It might mean starting a relationship with Jesus Christ, or showing up at a Celebrate Recovery meeting and dealing with your hurts, hang-ups, and habits. Whatever that next thing is for you, do it. It's time. Don't wait for tomorrow, don't wait for a sign, just do it.

You don't have to do it alone. Never forget you have a loving Father who wants to help you along your way. Call out to Jesus for help. Remember, he says, "Ask and it will be given to you; seek and you will find; knock and the door will be opened to you. For everyone who asks receives; the one who seeks finds; and to the one who knocks, the door will be opened" (Matt. 7:7–8). Jesus also says, "Come to me, all you who are weary and burdened, and I will give you rest. Take my yoke upon you and learn from me, for I am gentle and humble in heart, and you will find rest for your souls" (Matt. 11:28–29). Jesus wants to help you recover. You just have to ask him for help.

You also have people around you who want to help. We like to call Celebrate Recovery a Forever Family. We didn't get to choose the families we were born into, but we do get to choose a healthy family, one that will love us and be a safe port from life's storms. You can let Celebrate Recovery be that family. Oh, we are not a perfect family. We are a little bit strange. We are banged up and imperfect, but we know it, and weirdly we are proud of it! Some of us need a little extra grace, some of us are sandpaper people, and some of us are just a little off, but we love each other, and we love you. We are ready for you to come hang out with us. You don't have to go through recovery alone.

Take the next step. Do what you need to do. Keep moving forward and allow God to continue your recovery journey. I'm not stopping, and I hope you won't either.

Thank you so much for reading this book. I hope something in it has helped you in some way. If nothing else, I hope the Scripture was helpful. I know it was for me. As I sat behind this keyboard at my kitchen table and coffee shops, I was blown away by how God used his Word to teach me. I would encourage you to get into God's Word daily. Find a translation that is easy for you to read, such as the New International Version, which is my favorite.

Like I said, I'm not done in Celebrate Recovery by a long shot. God has a lot more to do in me, and I'm not ready to stop learning lessons yet. I hope some day I get to meet you at a Celebrate Recovery meeting, One Day Seminar, or Summit. If not, know two things. First, I'm praying for you. I'm praying that God will work in your life and give you freedom from whatever is holding you back. I'm praying that you will allow God and others to comfort you, and that you in turn will give back and comfort others as well. And second, I know that if you have trusted Jesus as your Lord and Savior, you and I are going to meet in heaven some-day at the biggest Celebrate Recovery party in the universe! We'll be able to praise Jesus face-to-face and tell each other about all of the amazing things he did in our lives and in the lives of those around us. That's going to be amazing.

See you on the journey.